MODERN AMERICAN DRINKS

How to Mix and Serve All Kinds of Cups and Drinks

BY

GEORGE J. KAPPELER

*A good drink at the proper time
Has a welcome in every clime*

SAALFIELD PUBLISHING CO.
NEW YORK   CHICAGO
1900

Historic Cookbooks of the World

COPYRIGHT, 1895
BY
GEORGE J. KAPPELER

"We could not now take time for further search or consideration, our victuals being much spent, especially our Beere."
— Mourt's Relation, 1622, attributed to William Bradford and Edward Winslow, on why Plymouth Rock was chosen.

Modern American Drinks: How to Serve All Kinds of Cups, Cocktails, and Fancy Mixed Drinks

© 2011 Compass Rose Technologies, Inc. All rights reserved. No part of this book may be reproduced in any manner whatsoever without written permission, except in the case of brief quotations embodied in critical articles and reviews. Originally published as *Modern American Drinks* by George J. Kappeler, 1895, 1900. Title page illustration courtesy of Dover Publications, Inc., New York.

Joanne Asala, Editor
Historic Cookbooks of the World

Rowan Grier, Series Editor
Classic Cocktail Guides
and Retro Bartender Books

Classic Cocktail Guides and Retro Bartender Books and *Historic Cookbooks of the World* are published by Kalevala Books, an imprint of Compass Rose Technologies, Inc., PO Box 409095, Chicago, IL 60640. Titles published by Kalevala Books are available at special quantity discounts to use as premiums and sales promotions or for academic use. For more information, please write to the Director of Special Sales, Compass Rose Technologies, Inc., PO Box 409095, Chicago, IL 60640. You may also contact us through our Web site, www.compassrose.com, or our blog, kalevalabooks.compassrose.com.

Editors' Note

Some ingredients found in vintage cocktail guides are unavailable or hard to come by today. Check out our resource guide at the back for vendors who specialize in hard-to-find ingredients and websites with information on how to recreate classic cocktails and cocktail ingredients.

ISBN: 978-1-880954-41-6

Classic Cocktail Guides
and Retro Bartender Books

Modern American Drinks

How to Mix and Serve All Kinds of Cups,
Cocktails, and Fancy Mixed Drinks

George J. Kappeler

Historic Cookbooks of the World
Kalevala Books, Chicago

PREFACE.

The recipes contained in this book are for the proper mixing of all kinds of drinks, such as Absinthes, Cocktails, Cups, Crustas, Cobblers, Coolers, Egg-Noggs, Fixes, Fizzes, Flips, Juleps, Lemonades, Punches, Pousse Café, Frozen Beverages, etc., etc. The formulas are simple, practical and easy to follow, and are especially intended for use in first-class Hotels, Clubs, Buffets, and Barrooms, where, if adopted and concocted according to directions given, they will be entirely satisfactory to the caterer and pleasing to the consumer, the latter of whom will immediately notice a marked improvement in his favorite beverage.

CONTENTS.

	PAGE
Absinthe	19
Absinthe, California Style	19
Absinthe Cocktail	28
Absinthe, Dripped	20
Absinthe Frappé, No. 1	64
Absinthe Frappé, No. 2	64
Absinthe, Italian Style	20
Absinthe, Swiss Style	20
Alderman's Nip	77
Ale Cup	48
Ale Flip	61
Ale Sangaree	99
Amaranth Cocktail	29
Ammonia and Seltzer	20
Ammonia, Soda, and Seltzer	21
Appetizer	21
Apple Brandy Cocktail	29
Apple Brandy Fix	56
Apple Brandy Punch	80
Apple Brandy Sour	103
Apple Toddy, Hot	68
Archbishop	21
Armour Cocktail	29
Arrack	21
Arrack Punch, Cold	81
Arrack Punch, Hot	68

CONTENTS.

	PAGE
Badminton Cup	48
Balaklava Cup	48
Baltimore Egg-Nogg	54
Barley Water	21
Beef Tea, Hot	69
Beef Tea, Frappé	106
Bicarbonate of Soda	22
Bishop	22
Black Stripe	22
Black Stripe, Hot	69
Blue Blazer	22
Boating-Club Punch	81
Boland Punch, Hot	81
Bonanza Punch	81
Bosom-Caresser	23
Boston Egg-Nogg	54
Bottled Cocktail, Brandy	29
Bottled Cocktail, Holland Gin	29
Bottled Cocktail, Tom Gin	30
Bottled Cocktail, Manhattan	30
Bottled Cocktail, Martini	30
Bottled Cocktail, Vermouth	30
Bottled Cocktail, Whiskey	30
Bracer	23
Brain-Duster	23
Brandy Champarelle	23
Brandy and Ginger Ale	23
Brandy and Gum	23
Brandy and Soda	23
Brandy and Sugar	23
Brandy Cocktail, Fancy	33
Brandy Cocktail, Old Fashion	33
Brandy Cocktail, Plain	33
Brandy Cobbler	26
Brandy Collins	44

Classic Cocktail Guides and Retro Bartender Books

CONTENTS.

	PAGE
Brandy Crusta	47
Brandy Daisy	53
Brandy Float	63
Brandy Fix	57
Brandy Flip	61
Brandy Fizz	57
Brandy Frappé	65
Brandy Julep	73
Brandy Punch	82
Brandy Punch, Frappé	64
Brandy Punch, Hot	69
Brandy Punch, Strained	82
Brandy Rickey	97
Brandy Sangaree	99
Brandy Scaffa	100
Brandy Sling, Cold	101
Brandy Sling, Hot	69
Brandy Smash, No. 1	102
Brandy Smash, No. 2	102
Brandy Sour	103
Brandy Toddy, Hot	69
Brandy Toddy, Cold	106
Brandy Toddy, Soft	107
Brandy Milk Punch	82
Brandy, Burned	24
Brandy and Peach, Burned	24
Brant Cocktail	33
Brunswick Cooler	45
Burgundy Cup, Red	49
Burgundy Cup, White	49
Café Parfait	78
Calasaya Cocktail	34
California Brandy Cobbler	26
California Sherry Cobbler	26
California Wine Cobbler	26

CONTENTS.

	PAGE
Canadian Cocktail	34
Canadian Club Punch	82
Canadian Rickey	97
Catawba Cobbler	27
Catawba Cooler	45
Century Club Punch	83
Country Cocktail	30
Champagne Cobbler	27
Champagne Cocktail	34
Champagne Cup, No. 1	49
Champagne Cup, No. 2	49
Champagne Julep	73
Champagne Punch	83
Champagne Punch, Fancy	83
Champagne Sour	104
Cherry Brandy	25
Chocolate Cocktail	34
Chocolate Punch	84
Cider Cocktail	34
Cider Cup	50
Cider Egg-Nog	54
Cider Fizz	58
Cider Nectar	78
Cider Punch	84
Cider Punch, Hot	70
Cincinnati	25
Clam Cocktail	35
Clam-Juice Cocktail	35
Claret Cobbler	27
Claret Cooler	45
Claret Cup	50
Claret Cup, English Style	51
Claret Cup, per glass	50
Claret Cup, à L'Anglais	51
Claret Punch	84

Classic Cocktail Guides and Retro Bartender Books

CONTENTS.

	PAGE
Claret and Seltzer	51
Club Punch	84
Coffee Cocktail	31
Coffee Frappé	65
Columbia Skin	101
Cooper	48
Cosmopolitan Punch	85
Curaçoa Float	64
Curaçoa Punch	85
Cupid	48
Continental Sour	104
Cordial Frappé	65
Domino Punch	85
Double-Barrel Cocktail	31
Dundorado Cocktail	31
Egg Flip	61
Electric Current Fizz	58
Egg-Nogg, Plain	55
Egg Phosphate	56
Egg Shake	56
Egg Sour	56
Eye-Opener	55
Fedora Punch	65
Fish House Punch	86
Floster	63
Ford Cocktail	31
French Café Royal	66
George Cocktail	32
Ginger Ale Cooler	45
Ginger Ale Daisy	53
Gin and Pine	67
Gin and Tansy	67
Gin and Wormwood	67
Gin Cocktail, Holland	32
Gin Cocktail, Old Fashion	32

CONTENTS.

	PAGE
Gin Cocktail, Plymouth	35
Gin Cocktail, Schiedam	35
Gin Cocktail, Tom	35
Gin Cocktail, Tom, Old Fashioned	35
Gin Crusta	47
Gin Daisy	53
Gin Fix	57
Gin Fizz, Plain	58
Gin Flip	62
Gin Julep	73
Gin Milk Punch	86
Gin Puff	86
Gin Punch	86
Gin Punch, Hot	70
Gin Rickey	97
Gin Sangaree	99
Gin Sling, Cold,	101
Gin Sling, Hot	70
Gin Smash, On Ice	103
Gin Smash, Strained	102
Gin Sour	104
Gin, Spiced, Hot	70
Gin Tea Punch	86
Gin Toddy, Cold	107
Gin Toddy, Soft	107
Glee Club Punch	87
Glasgow Flip	62
Golden Flip	62
Golden Fizz	58
Golden Slipper	67
Grenadine Cocktail	36
Grenadine Lemonade	67
Gum Syrup	106
Half and Half, American Style	68
Half and Half, English Style	68

CONTENTS.

	PAGE
Hancock Punch	87
Hari-Kari	68
Harvard Cocktail	36
Heidsieck Cup	51
Hiram Cocktail	36
Holland House Cocktail	32
Horse's Neck	68
Horsford Punch	87
Imperial Punch	88
India Cup (per glass)	52
Inimitable Cocktail	36
Irish Cocktail, No. 1	36
Irish Cocktail, No. 2	37
Irish Punch	88
Irish Punch, Hot	70
Irish Sling, Hot	70
Italian Wine Lemonade	77
Jamaica Rum Cocktail	37
Jamaica Rum Flip	62
Jamaica Rum Punch	88
Jamaica Rum Punch, Hot	71
Jamaica Rum, Hot, Spiced	71
Jamaica Rum Sling, Hot	71
Japanese Punch	88
Jersey Cocktail	37
Jersey Sour	104
John Collins	44
Kentucky Flip, Hot	71
Kentucky Toddy	107
Kirsch Punch, Fancy	88
Kirschwasser Punch	88
Knickerbein	74
Knickerbocker	74
Knickerbocker Punch	88
Lalla Rookh	74

CONTENTS.

	PAGE
Lemonade, Angostura	75
Lemonade, Claret	25
Lemonade, Egg	75
Lemonade, Hot	71
Lemonade, Lime	77
Lemonade, Phosphate	76
Lemonade, Plain	76
Lemonade, Rhine Wine	76
Lemonade, Seltzer	76
Lemonade, Soda	76
Lemonade, Tea	77
Lemon Squash	75
Lemon Syrup	75
Liberal Cocktail	87
Lime Gin Fizz	58
Lincoln Club Cooler	46
Lincoln Club Cup	52
Long-Range Cocktail	37
Locomotive, Hot	71
Manhattan Cocktail	38
Manhattan Cocktail, Dry	38
Manhattan Cocktail, Extra Dry	38
Manhattan Punch	89
Martini Cocktail	38
Marmora Cup	52
Medford Rum Cocktail	39
Medford Rum Punch	90
Medford Rum Smash	103
Medford Rum Sour	104
Metropole Cocktail	39
Metropolitan Cocktail	39
Mikado Punch	90
Milk Punch	90
Milk Punch, Hot	72
Mint Julep, Southern Style	74

Classic Cocktail Guides and Retro Bartender Books

CONTENTS.

	PAGE
Mississippi Punch	90
Mountain Cocktail	39
Morning Glory Fizz	59
Mulled Ale, English Style	55
Mulled Claret	25
Mulled Claret and Egg	25
National Punch	91
Negus, Port Wine	78
Negus, Sherry Wine	78
New Orleans Fizz	59
New Orleans, Pousse Café	79
Orangeade	78
Orange Punch	91
Orgeat Punch	91
Oyster Cocktail	39
Peach and Honey	80
Peach Blow	80
Peach Punch	80
Pepsin Cocktail	40
Pick Me Up	80
Pistache Fizz	59
Poland Punch	92
Port Wine Cobbler	27
Port Wine Flip	62
Port Wine Punch	92
Port Wine Sangaree	99
Pousse Café, American	79
Pousse Café, French	79
Pousse Café, Jersey Lily	76
Pousse l'Amour	80
Princeton Cocktail	40
Presidential Punch	92
Racquet Club Cocktail	40
Ramsay Cooler	46
Raspberry Cream Frappé	66

CONTENTS.

	PAGE
Raspberry Syrup	106
Raspberry Vinegar	109
Rebb. Davis Punch	92
Remmsen Cooler	46
Renwick Cooler	46
Reviver	97
Rhine Wine Cobbler	27
Rhine Wine Punch	93
Rhine Wine and Seltzer	98
Riding Club Cocktail	40
Robinson Cocktail	41
Rocky Mountain Cooler	46
Rock and Rye	98
Roman Punch	93
Royal Cup	52
Royal Fizz	59
Ruby Punch	93
Rum Daisy	53
Rum Flip	63
Rum and Gum	98
Rum and Sugar	98
Russian Punch	93
Russian Tea Punch	94
Sam Ward	91
Saratoga Cocktail	41
Sauterne Cobbler	28
Sauterne Cup	53
Sauterne Fizz	60
Sauterne Punch	94
Schickler	100
Scotch Whiskey and Soda	100
Scotch Whiskey Rickey	98
Scotch Whiskey Skin	101
Scotch Whiskey Sling	102
Scotch Whiskey, Hot	72

Classic Cocktail Guides and Retro Bartender Books

CONTENTS.

	PAGE
Scotch Whiskey Punch, Cold	94
Scotch Whiskey Punch, Hot	72
Shandy Gaff	100
Sherry Cobbler, No. 1	28
Sherry Cobbler, No. 2	28
Sherry and Bitters	100
Sherry and Egg	101
Sherry Egg-Nogg	55
Sherry Egg-Nogg, Fancy	55
Sherry Flip	63
Sherry Punch	94
Sherry Sangaree	99
Siberian Punch	95
Silver Fizz	60
Smith Cocktail	41
Snowball	103
Soda Cocktail	41
Soda Fizz	60
Southern Cooler	46
Southern Toddy	107
Split Turkay	105
Star Cocktail	41
St. Charles Punch	95
St. Croix Crusta	49
St. Croix Fix	57
St. Croix Fizz	60
St. Croix Rum Punch	95
St. Croix Sour	104
Steinway Punch	95
Stone Fence	105
Stone Wall	105
Syllabub	105
Tam o' Shanter	105
Tailor's Fizz	61
Tip-Top Punch	96

CONTENTS.

	PAGE
Tom Collins	45
Tom and Jerry Mixture	108
Tom and Jerry (how to serve)	108
Tom and Jerry, Cold	108
Turf Cocktail	42
Union Cocktail	42
Vanilla Punch	96
Velvet	108
Vermouth and Bitters	109
Vermouth Cocktail	42
Vermouth Cocktail, Dry	42
Vermouth Cocktail, Fancy	42
Vermouth Cocktail, French	43
Vermouth Frappé, French	66
Vermouth Frappé, Italian	66
Vermouth Rickey	98
Violet Fizz	61
Wassail Bowl	109
West Indian Punch	96
Widow's Kiss	110
Whiskey Cobbler	28
Whiskey Cocktail	43
Whiskey Cocktail, Fancy	43
Whiskey Cocktail, Old Fashion	43
Whiskey Crusta	47
Whiskey Daisy	54
Whiskey Fix	57
Whiskey Fizz	61
Whiskey Flip	63
Whiskey Julep	74
Whiskey Rickey	99
Whiskey Skin	101
Whiskey Sling, Cold	102
Whiskey Sling, Hot	72
Whiskey Smash	103

Classic Cocktail Guides and Retro Bartender Books

CONTENTS.

	PAGE
Whiskey Sour	104
Whiskey Toddy (Cold)	108
Whiskey Punch, Plain	96
Whiskey Punch, Hot	73
Whiskey Punch, Frappé	66
Whiskey Punch, Strained	97
White Lion	77
White Plush	109
Wilson Cocktail	43
Yale Cocktail	44
Yale Punch	97
Yankee Flip	68
York Cocktail	44

FROZEN BEVERAGES.

Blackberry Sherbet	119
Bonanza Punch	113
Cherry Sherbet	119
Café Royal, Frappé	120
Currant Sherbet, No. 1	119
Currant Sherbet, No. 2	120
Egg-Nogg, Frappé	114
Grape Sherbet	114
Kirsch Punch	114
Lemon Ice	111
Lemon Sherbet	114
Lemon Ginger Sherbet	115
Macedoine, No. 1	117
Macedoine, No. 2	117
Macedoine, No. 3	117
Macedoine, No. 4	117
Orange Ice	112
Orange Sherbet, No. 1	117
Orange Sherbet, No. 2	118

CONTENTS.

	PAGE
Pineapple Ice	112
Pineapple Sherbet	118
Pomegranate Sherbet	115
Punch à la Vatican	116
Raspberry Water Ice	113
Raspberry Sherbet	116
Roman Punch	118
Russian Punch	119
Shaddock Sherbet	116
Strawberry Sherbet	117
Strawberry Water Ice	112
Tea Punch, Frappé	114
Water Ice	113

MODERN AMERICAN DRINKS.

Absinthe.

Absinthe is composed of the tops and leaves of the herb artemisia absinthium, or wormwood, which contains a volatile oil, absinthol, and a yellow, crystalline, resinous compound, called absinthin, which is the bitter principle. The alcohol with which this is mixed holds these volatile oils in solution.

The free use of absinthe is injurious. Never serve it in any kind of drink unless called for by the customer.

California Style Absinthe.

A mixing-glass* half full fine ice, one jigger absinthe. Shake until very cold, strain into thin bar-glass, fill with siphon seltzer or carbonic.

---

* By a mixing-glass is meant a large soda-glass, holding twelve ounces; it is handier and gives better satisfaction than a goblet. A jigger is a measure used for measuring liquors when mixing drinks; it holds two ounces. A pony holds half a jigger.

Dripped Absinthe.

(Use Absinthe Drip-glass.)

Pour one pony of absinthe into the bottom glass, fill the upper (drip) glass full of ice-water. When two-thirds of the water has dripped into the absinthe it is ready to be drunk. A few drops of anisette will improve this drink.

Absinthe, Italian Style.

Put into a thin eight-ounce glass containing a few lumps of clear ice one pony of absinthe, two dashes maraschino, four dashes anisette. Slowly fill the glass with ice-water, stir well with long bar-spoon. Serve.

Absinthe, Swiss Style.

Fill a mixing-glass half-full of fine ice, pour into it one pony of absinthe, one pony of water, one dash of gum-syrup. Shake with shaker until very cold, strain into champagne-tumbler, fill up with siphon seltzer.

Ammonia and Seltzer.

This is a good remedy for the relief of the depression following alcoholic excesses. Dose: Twenty drops of spirit. ammon. aromat. in a medium-sized glass of seltzer or plain water.

Ammonia, Soda, and Seltzer.

Same as ammonia and seltzer, mixing a small bar-spoonful of bicarbonate of soda in the drink before imbibing.

Archbishop.

Dissolve in a mixing-glass one-half tablespoonful fine sugar in a little water, the juice of quarter of a lemon, fill glass half-full fine ice, add one jigger port wine, two dashes Jamaica rum. Shake well. Serve in long thin punch-glass on ice with straws. Trim with fruit in season.

Arrack.

Arrack is made from the juice obtained from the cocoanut-tree. There is another kind made from rice. That which is imported from Japan is considered the best.

Appetizer.

A mixing-glass half-full fine ice; add three dashes absinthe, three dashes pepsin bitters, one jigger French vermouth. Shake well, strain, and serve.

Barley Water.

One tablespoonful pearl barley to two quarts water. Put on fire and boil two minutes; strain through cheesecloth. This makes an excellent drink if made into lemonade.

Bicarbonate of Soda.

One small bar-spoonful of bicarbonate of soda in a medium-sized glassful of plain water or seltzer (this is an excellent stomach-settler).

Black Stripe.

One teaspoonful molasses, one small lump ice, one jigger Jamaica, Medford, or St. Croix rum. Mix well in small bar-glass. Serve.

Bishop.

A long thin punch-glass half-full fine ice, the juice of quarter of a lemon, the juice of half an orange, one dash Jamaica rum, two jiggers Burgundy, one tablespoonful fine sugar. Mix well, fill the glass with seltzer, ornament with fruit. Serve straws.

Blue Blazer.

One lump of sugar dissolved with a little hot water in a mug; add one jigger of Scotch whiskey. Ignite this mixture. Take another mug and pour from one to the other several times, giving it the appearance of a streak of blue fire. Serve in hot-drink glass. Add a piece twisted lemon-peel and a little grated nutmeg.

Bosom Caresser.

Fill a mixing-glass one-third full of fine ice; add a teaspoonful raspberry syrup, one fresh egg, one jigger brandy; fill with milk, shake well, and strain.

Bracer.

One pony brandy, one-half pony yellow chartreuse, one-half pony maraschino, five drops absinthe, the yolk of one egg whipped, one tablespoonful fine sugar. Mix well with ice, strain, and serve in small fancy glasses.

Brain-Duster.

A mixing-glass half-full of fine ice, two dashes gum syrup, one pony absinthe, one-half pony Italian vermouth, one-half pony whiskey. Mix well, strain into thin glass, fill with seltzer.

Brandy and Ginger Ale.

Place a lump of ice in a long thin punch-glass, add one jigger brandy and a cold bottle of imported ginger ale.

Brandy Champerelle.

Fill a sherry-glass one-fourth full maraschino, one-fourth full orange curacoa, one-fourth full yellow chartreuse, and one-fourth full brandy. Add a few drops of Angostura bitters carefully. Be sure to keep the different liqueurs from running into one another.

Brandy and Gum.

A few dashes gum-syrup in a whiskey-glass, one lump ice, a small bar-spoon. Place, with a decanter of brandy, before customer, to help himself.

Brandy and Soda.

One lump of ice in long punchglass, one jigger brandy, one bottle cold soda.

Brandy and Sugar.

One lump of sugar dissolved with a little water in a whiskey-glass, one lump ice, a small bar-spoon. Place, with a decanter of brandy, before customer.

Burned Brandy.
(GOOD IN A CASE OF DIARRHŒA.)

Put two lumps of cut-loaf sugar in a dish; add one jigger good brandy, and ignite. When sufficiently burnt, serve in a whiskey-glass.

Burned Brandy and Peach.

Prepare same as Burned Brandy. Place two or three slices of dried peaches in the glass, pour the burned liquid over them, grate a little nutmeg on top. Serve.

Classic Cocktail Guides and Retro Bartender Books

Cincinnati.

A glass half-full of lemon soda; then fill with draught beer.

Cherry Brandy.

Ten pounds of ripe wild cherries are freed from their pits, the pits are pulverized, and, with the cherries and one gallon brandy, placed in a demijohn or a covered stone jar for eight weeks. Add two pounds refined sugar, filter through filtering-paper, bottle; but use only after it has been bottled at least six weeks.

Claret Lemonade.

Make a plain, sweet lemonade, add a jigger of claret before shaking; decorate with fruit. Serve straws.

Mulled Claret.

Put in a dish four lumps sugar, two jiggers claret, the juice of a quarter of a lemon, a little powdered allspice, three cloves, a small stick cinnamon. Bring the above to the boiling point, then strain into a hot-drink glass, and add a slice of lemon.

Mulled Claret and Egg.

Prepare same as Mulled Claret, leaving out the lump sugar. Boil the mixture one minute. Beat up the yolk of one egg with a small spoonful of fine sugar. Place the beaten egg in a hot-drink glass and pour the boiling claret over it, mixing well with spoon; grate a little nutmeg on top.

Brandy Cobbler.

Fill a thin fizz-glass three-fourths full of fine ice, add three dashes gum-syrup, three dashes maraschino, one jigger brandy. Mix well. Trim with fruit in season. Serve with straws.

California Brandy Cobbler.

Prepare same as Brandy Cobbler, using California brandy.

California Sherry Cobbler.

Two tablespoonfuls fine sugar in a mixing-glass with a little water, the juice of one orange, two jiggers California sherry; fill the glass with fine ice, shake well, put all into a long thin glass, trim with fruit. Serve straws.

California Wine Cobbler.

Dissolve two tablespoonfuls fine sugar with a little water in a mixing-glass. Add the juice of one orange, two jiggers California wine; fill the glass three-fourths with fine ice, shake well. Serve in a long thin glass with straws. Ornament with fruit in season.

Catawba Cobbler.

One tablespoonful fine sugar, the juice of half a lemon, two jiggers of Catawba wine in half a glass (mixing) full fine ice; shake well. Trim with fruit. Sip with straws.

Champagne Cobbler.

Dissolve one lump sugar in a long thin glass with a little water, add a piece of lemon-peel, a slice of orange, a few lumps ice, then fill with champagne; stir. Sip with straws.

Claret Cobbler.

One-half tablespoonful fine sugar in a mixing-glass three-fourths full of fine ice, two jiggers claret; shake well. Trim with fruit. Serve with straws in a long thin glass.

Port Wine Cobbler.

A thin eight-ounce glassful fine ice, one tablespoonful gum-syrup, one jigger port wine. Mix well. Ornament with fruit. Serve straws.

Rhine Wine Cobbler.

Dissolve one tablespoonful fine sugar with one jigger water in a long thin glass. Add two jiggers Rhine wine; fill the glass with fine ice; mix well. Trim with fruit. Serve straws.

Sauterne Cobbler.

One tablespoonful fine sugar dissolved in a long thin glass with a little water; fill the glass with fine ice, add two jiggers sauterne. Mix. Ornament with fruits in season. Sip with straws.

Sherry Cobbler No. 1.

Fill an eight-ounce glass full of fine ice, add one teaspoonful gum-syrup, two jiggers sherry. Mix well. Trim with fruit. Serve with straws.

Sherry Cobbler No. 2.

Half a mixing-glass full fine ice, one tablespoonful fine sugar, one and a half jigger sherry wine. Shake well. Serve in a long thin glass with straws. Trim with fruit.

Whiskey Cobbler.

Prepare the same as Brandy Cobbler, substituting whiskey for brandy.

Absinthe Cocktail.

Fill a mixing-glass half-full of fine ice, add one dash gum-syrup, one dash Peyschaud or Angostura bitters, one pony absinthe, one pony water. Mix well. Strain into cocktail glass; add a piece twisted lemon-peel.

Amaranth Cocktail.

Fine ice in a mixing-glass, two dashes Angostura bitters, one jigger whiskey. Mix, strain into a whiskey-glass, and fill up with seltzer; then take a very little fine sugar in a small bar-spoon and stir into the cocktail. Drink during effervescence.

Apple Brandy Cocktail.

A mixing-glass half-full fine ice, two dashes Peyschaud or Angostura bitters, one jigger apple brandy. Mix and strain into a cocktail-glass. Add a piece of twisted lemon-peel.

Armour Cocktail.

Fine ice in mixing-glass, three dashes orange bitters, half a jigger sherry, half a jigger Italian vermouth. Mix, strain into cocktail-glass. Add a piece of orange-peel or a maraschino cherry.

Bottled Brandy Cocktail.

Take two-thirds of a quart brandy, one-third quart water, one pony Peyschaud or Angostura bitters, two ponies gum-syrup. Mix well and bottle.

Bottled Holland Gin Cocktail.

Prepare same as Bottled Brandy Cocktail, substituting Holland gin for brandy.

Bottled Tom Gin Cocktail.

Two-thirds of a quart Tom gin, one-third quart water, one jigger orange bitters. Mix well and bottle.

Bottled Whiskey Cocktail.

Prepare same as Brandy Bottled Cocktail, using whiskey in place of brandy.

Bottled Martini Cocktail.

Take one-third quart Tom gin, one-third quart Italian vermouth, one-third quart water. Add one jigger orange bitters. Mix well and bottle.

Bottled Manhattan Cocktail.

One-third of a quart of whiskey, one-third Italian vermouth, one-third water. Add one and a half pony Peyschaud or Angostura bitters, one pony gum-syrup. Mix well and bottle.

Bottled Vermouth Cocktail.

Three-fourths vermouth, one-fourth water, one and a half pony bitters. Mix and bottle. If desired sweet, add gum-syrup to taste.

Country Cocktail.

A mixing-glass half-full fine ice, two dashes of orange bitters, two dashes Boker bitters, one piece lemon-peel, one jigger rye whiskey—no sweetening. Mix and strain into a cocktail-glass.

Coffee Cocktail.

Fill a mixing-glass half-full fine ice, add two dashes Angostura bitters, half a tablespoonful fine sugar, one fresh egg, half a jigger port wine, half a jigger brandy. Shake well. Strain into a large cocktail-glass. Add a piece of twisted lemon-peel.

Double-Barrel Cocktail.

Mixing-glass half-full fine ice, two dashes Angostura bitters, two dashes orange bitters, one-third jigger French vermouth, one-third jigger Italian vermouth, one-third jigger whiskey. Mix and strain into cocktail-glass.

Dundorado Cocktail.

One-half jigger Tom gin, one-half jigger Italian vermouth, a mixing-glass half-full fine ice, two dashes calasaya. Mix and strain into cocktail-glass.

Ford Cocktail.

Three dashes benedictine, three dashes orange bitters, half a jigger Tom gin, half a jigger French vermouth. Mix in a mixing-glass half-full fine ice. Strain into a cocktail-glass. Add a piece twisted orange-peel.

George Cocktail.

A GOOD APPETIZER.

Mixing-glass half-full fine ice, three dashes pepsin bitters, one jigger Tom gin. Mix and strain into cocktail-glass. Add a piece of twisted lemon-peel.

Holland Gin Cocktail.

Mixing-glass half-full fine ice, two dashes Angostura bitters or Peyschaud bitters, two dashes gum-syrup, one jigger Holland gin. Mix; strain into a cocktail-glass. Add a piece of twisted lemon-peel or a maraschino cherry.

Old-Fashioned Holland Gin Cocktail.

Crush a small lump of sugar in a whiskey-glass containing a little water, add a lump of ice, two dashes of Angostura bitters, a small piece of lemon peel, one jigger Holland gin. Mix with small bar-spoon. Serve.

Holland House Cocktail.

Mixing-glass half-full fine ice, two dashes Peyschaud bitters, one-half pony Eau de Vie d'Oranges, one and a half pony old rye whiskey, a piece lemon-peel. Mix. Moisten the edge of cocktail-glass with lemon, dip in sugar. Strain the cocktail into the prepared glass.

Classic Cocktail Guides and Retro Bartender Books

Brandy Cocktail.

A mixing-glass half-full fine ice, two dashes gum-syrup, two dashes Peyschaud or Angostura bitters, one jigger brandy. Mix and strain into cocktail-glass. Add a piece twisted lemon-peel or a maraschino cherry.

Fancy Brandy Cocktail.

Fill a mixing-glass half-full fine ice, add three dashes maraschino, two dashes Peyschaud or Angostura bitters, one jigger brandy, one dash orange bitters. Mix. Strain into fancy cocktail-glass, the rim of which has been moistened with a piece of lemon and dipped in powdered sugar, which gives it the appearance of being frosted.

Old-Fashioned Brandy Cocktail.

Crush a small lump of sugar in a whiskey-glass with a very little water, add one lump ice, two dashes bitters, a small piece-lemon peel, one jigger brandy. Stir with small bar-spoon. Serve.

Brant Cocktail.

Mixing-glass half-full fine ice, two dashes Angostura bitters, one-third of a jigger white crème de menthe, two-thirds of a jigger brandy. Mix well. Strain into cocktail-glass; twist a piece of lemon-peel over the top.

Calasaya Cocktail.

Half a jigger calasaya, half a jigger whiskey, one small piece lemon-peel, half a mixing-glass full fine ice. Mix well and strain into a cocktail-glass.

Canadian Cocktail.

Prepare same as Whiskey Cocktail, using Canadian whiskey.

Champagne Cocktail.

Put into a long thin glass one lump cut-loaf sugar saturated with Peyschaud or Angostura bitters, add one lump of ice, a small piece of lemon-peel; fill the glass three-fourths full cold champagne. Stir with spoon and serve.

Chocolate Cocktail.

Break a fresh egg into a mixing-glass, half full fine ice, add one dash bitters, one jigger port wine, one teaspoonful fine sugar. Shake well and strain into a cocktail-glass.

Cider Cocktail.

Saturate a lump of cut-loaf sugar with Angostura bitters. Place it, with one lump of ice and a small piece of lemon peel, in a thin cider-glass, then fill up with cold cider. Stir with spoon and serve.

Classic Cocktail Guides and Retro Bartender Books

Clam Cocktail.

Put into a large cocktail-glass a half-dozen little-neck clams with all their liquor, season with pepper and salt to taste; add two dashes lemon-juice, one dash Tobasco sauce, and a very little cayenne pepper.

Clam Juice Cocktail.

Two jiggers clam juice in a thin bar-glass, season same as Clam Cocktail.

Plymouth Gin Cocktail.

Mixing-glass half-full fine ice, three dashes Peyschaud or orange bitters, one jigger Plymouth gin. Mix well, strain into cocktail-glass. Add a small piece lemon-peel or a maraschino cherry.

Schiedam Gin Cocktail.

Mix same as Holland Gin Cocktail, using Schiedam gin in place of Holland.

Tom Gin Cocktail.

Prepare same as Plymouth Gin Cocktail, substituting Old Tom gin for Plymouth.

Old-Fashioned Tom Gin Cocktail.

Mix same as Holland Gin Old-Fashioned Cocktail, using Old Tom gin in place of Holland.

Grenadine Cocktail.

Use Grenadine in place of gum-syrup in any kind of cocktail.

Harvard Cocktail.

One dash gum-syrup, three dashes Angostura bitters, half-jigger Italian vermouth, half-jigger brandy in half a mixing-glass of fine ice. Mix, strain into cocktail-glass, fill up with seltzer.

Hiram Cocktail.

A mixing-glass half-full fine ice, two dashes Peyschaud bitters, one-half jigger Italian vermouth, one-half jigger Walker Canadian whiskey. Mix, strain into cocktail-glass; add a maraschino cherry.

Inimitable Cocktail.

Dissolve a small lump of sugar with a little water in a whiskey-glass, add one lump of ice, one dash lemon-juice, two dashes Peyschaud bitters, one jigger Tom gin. Mix with small barspoon. Serve.

Irish Cocktail No. 1.

Mixing-glass half-full fine ice, three dashes orange bitters, two dashes acid phosphate, one-half jigger whiskey, one-half jigger Italian vermouth. Mix well, strain into cocktail-glass.

Irish Cocktail No. 2.

Two dashes gum-syrup, three dashes Angostura bitters in a mixing-glass with fine ice, one jigger Irish whiskey. Mix, strain, and add a piece twisted lemon-peel.

Jamaica Rum Cocktail.

Mixing-glass half-full fine ice, two dashes gum-syrup, two dashes orange bitters, two dashes Angostura bitters, one jigger Jamaica rum. Mix and strain into cocktail-glass. Add a small piece twisted lemon-peel.

Jersey Cocktail.

One-half tablespoonful fine sugar in a thin cider-glass, add one lump of ice, two dashes Angostura bitters, one piece lemon-peel, fill up with cider. Stir well. Drink while effervescent.

Liberal Cocktail.

Fill a mixing-glass half-full fine ice, add one dash syrup, half a jigger Amer Picon bitters, half a jigger whiskey. Mix, strain into cocktail-glass. A small piece of lemon peel on top. Serve.

Long-Range Cocktail.

Mixing-glass half-full fine ice, two dashes gum-syrup, two dashes Peyschaud bitters, one pony

Italian vermouth, half a pony absinthe, half a pony brandy. Mix and strain into cocktail-glass. Twist a piece lemon-peel over top.

Manhattan Cocktail.

Fill mixing-glass half-full fine ice, add two dashes gum-syrup, two dashes Peyschaud or Angostura bitters, one half-jigger Italian vermouth, one-half jigger whiskey. Mix, strain into cocktail-glass. Add a piece of lemon-peel or a cherry.

Manhattan Cocktail, Dry.

Prepare same as Manhattan Cocktail, leaving out syrup and cherry.

Manhattan Cocktail, Extra Dry.

Mix same as Manhattan cocktail. Leave out syrup and cherry, and use French vermouth in place of Italian.

Martini Cocktail.

Half a mixing-glass full fine ice, three dashes orange bitters, one-half jigger Tom gin, one-half jigger Italian vermouth, a piece lemon-peel. Mix, strain into cocktail-glass. Add a maraschino cherry, if desired by customer.

Medford Rum Cocktail.

Prepare same as Brandy Cocktail, using Medford rum in place of brandy.

Metropole Cocktail.

Two dashes gum-syrup, two dashes Peyschaud bitters, one dash orange bitters, half a jigger brandy, half a jigger French vermouth, a mixing-glass half-full fine ice. Mix, strain into cocktail-glass, add a maraschino cherry.

Metropolitan Cocktail.

Two lumps of ice in a small wine-glass, add three dashes gum-syrup, two dashes Angostura bitters, one pony brandy, one pony French vermouth. Mix, take out the ice, add a small piece twisted lemon-peel.

Mountain Cocktail.

A cocktail-glass half-full hard cider, one fresh egg; season with pepper and salt. Serve.

Oyster Cocktail.

A few dashes lemon-juice in a tumbler, add a dash of Tobasco sauce, a teaspoonful of vinegar, a few dashes tomato catchup, six Blue Point oysters, with all their liquor; season to taste with pepper and salt. Mix and serve with spoon in the glass.

Pepsin Cocktail.

Fill mixing-glass half-full fine ice, three dashes gum-syrup, five dashes pepsin bitters, one jigger whiskey. Mix, strain into cocktail-glass, add piece twisted lemon-peel.

Princeton Cocktail.

A mixing-glass half-full fine ice, three dashes orange bitters, one and a half pony Tom gin. Mix, strain into cocktail-glass; add half a pony port wine carefully and let it settle in bottom of cocktail before serving.

Racquet Club Cocktail.

Three dashes orange bitters, half a jigger Tom gin, half a jigger French vermouth, in a mixing-glass half-full fine ice. Mix, strain into cocktail-glass, add piece twisted lemon-peel.

Riding Club Cocktail.

Mixing-glass half-full fine ice, one dash Angostura bitters, a small bar-spoonful Horsford acid phosphate, one jigger calasaya. Mix and strain into cocktail-glass.

Robinson Cocktail.

Mixing-glass half-full fine ice, three dashes Peyschaud bitters, one piece lemon-peel, one jigger Bourbon whiskey; shake until very cold. Strain into cocktail-glass. Never use sweetening in this drink.

Saratoga Cocktail.

Prepare in the same manner as a Fancy Brandy cocktail. Before serving add a squirt of champagne.

Smith Cocktail.

Fill mixing-glass half-full fine ice, add three dashes Angostura bitters, one-half jigger Holland gin, one-half jigger French vermouth; shake until cold. Strain into cocktail-glass; twist a small piece lemon-peel on top.

Soda Cocktail.

One teaspoonful fine sugar in a large barglass, one lump of ice, three dashes Angostura bitters, one piece lemon-peel; add one bottle of plain or lemon soda. Mix and drink during effervescence.

Star Cocktail.

Fill a mixing-glass half-full fine ice, add two dashes gum-syrup, three dashes Peyschaud or Angostura bitters, one-half jigger apple brandy, one-half jigger Italian vermouth. Mix, strain into cocktail-glass, twist small piece lemon-peel on top.

Turf Cocktail.

One dash Angostura bitters, three dashes orange bitters, one jigger Tom gin in a mixing-glass half-full fine ice. Mix, strain into cocktail-glass; add a piece twisted lemon-peel.

Union Cocktail.

One lump ice in a whiskey-glass; add one dash Peyschaud bitters, two dashes orange bitters, one small piece lemon-peel, one jigger Tom gin. Mix with small bar-spoon. Serve.

Vermouth Cocktail.

Mixing-glass half-full fine ice, two dashes Angostura or Peyschaud bitters, one jigger Italian vermouth. Mix well, strain into cocktail-glass; add a piece lemon-peel or cherry.

Vermouth Cocktail, Dry.

Prepare same as Vermouth Cocktail, using French vermouth in place of Italian; twist a piece lemon-peel over top. Leave out the cherry.

Fancy Vermouth Cocktail.

Mix same as Fancy Brandy Cocktail, substituting vermouth for brandy.

French Vermouth Cocktail.

Three dashes orange bitters in mixing-glass half full fine ice; add one jigger French vermouth. Mix well, strain into cocktail-glass; add a piece twisted lemon-peel on top.

Whiskey Cocktail.

Mixing-glass half-full fine ice, two dashes gum-syrup, two dashes Angostura or Peyschaud bitters, one jigger whiskey. Mix, strain into cocktail-glass; add a small piece of twisted lemon-peel or a cherry.

Fancy Whiskey Cocktail.

Prepare in the same manner as Fancy Brandy Cocktail, substituting whiskey for brandy.

Old-Fashioned Whiskey Cocktail.

Dissolve a small lump of sugar with a little water in a whiskey-glass; add two dashes Angostura bitters, a small piece ice, a piece lemon-peel, one jigger whiskey. Mix with small bar-spoon and serve, leaving spoon in the glass.

Wilson Cocktail.

Mix same as Whiskey Cocktail, using Wilson whiskey.

Yale Cocktail.

Fill a mixing-glass half-full fine ice, three dashes orange bitters, one dash Peyschaud bitters, a piece lemon-peel, one jigger Tom gin. Mix, strain into cocktail-glass; add a squirt of siphon seltzer.

York Cocktail.

A mixing-glass half-full fine ice, three dashes orange bitters, one-half jigger whiskey, one-half jigger vermouth. Mix, strain into cocktail-glass, squeeze piece of lemon-peel over the top. Serve.

Brandy Collins.

Cut a lemon in half, place it in a mixing-glass, add one tablespoonful fine sugar, crush with muddler so as to extract both the juice of the lemon and part of the oil of the rind, fill the glass half full of fine ice, add one jigger brandy. Mix well, strain into a Collins-glass containing a piece of ice, pour in a bottle of plain soda. Stir with a long bar-spoon and serve.

John Collins.

Prepare same as Brandy Collins, substituting Holland gin for brandy.

Tom Collins.

Is prepared in the same manner as John Collins, using Tom gin in place of Holland gin.

Catawba Cooler.

Pare a lemon so as to leave the rind in one spiral-shaped piece. Place a piece of ice inside the rind, put both into a long Collins-glass, add one and a half jigger Catawba wine and a cold bottle of plain soda. Stir and serve.

Brunswick Cooler.

The juice of one lemon, the rind of a lemon, same as for Catawba Cooler, half a tablespoonful fine sugar in a long glass. Mix, add a bottle of imported ginger ale. Stir and serve.

Claret Cooler.

Prepare same as Catawba Cooler, using claret in place of catawba.

Ginger Ale Cooler.

Is prepared in the same manner as Brunswick Cooler, but you can use domestic ginger ale if you wish.

Lincoln Club Cooler.

Take a long thin Collins-glass, put into it one lump of ice, one pony St. Croix rum, fill up with a cold bottle imported ginger ale. Serve.

Ramsay Cooler.

Prepare in the same manner as Catawba Cooler, using one jigger of Scotch whiskey in place of Catawba wine.

Remmsen Cooler.

Mix and serve same as Ramsay Cooler, substituting Old Tom gin for Scotch whiskey.

Renwick Cooler.

The peel of a lemon, same as for Ramsay Cooler, one piece of ice, put into a Collins-glass; add one jigger whiskey and one bottle of imported ginger ale. Stir and serve.

Rocky Mountain Cooler.

Beat up one egg with one tablespoonful fine sugar and the juice of half a lemon, fill up with cider; stir well. Serve in a long thin glass. Grate nutmeg on top.

Southern Cooler.

The rind of a whole lemon, a piece of ice in a Collins-glass; add half a jigger Jamaica rum, half a jigger Bourbon whiskey, one teaspoonful fine sugar, one bottle cold plain soda. Stir with long barspoon. Drink during effervescence.

Brandy Crusta.

Fill a mixing-glass half full of fine ice; add three dashes of gum-syrup, two dashes maraschino, the juice of a quarter of a lemon, two dashes Peyschaud or Angostura bitters, and one jigger brandy; mix. Take a lemon the size of a fancy sauterne or claret glass; peel the rind from three-fourths of it all in one piece; fit it into the glass; moisten the edge of the glass with a piece of lemon, and dip it into fine sugar, which gives it a frosted appearance. Strain your mixture into this glass, trim with fruit, and serve.

Gin Crusta.

Prepare same as Brandy Crusta, substituting gin for brandy.

St. Croix Crusta.

Mix and serve same as Brandy Crusta, using St. Croix rum in place of brandy.

Whiskey Crusta.

Is prepared in the same manner as Brandy Crusta, substituting the desired kind of whiskey for brandy.

Cooper.

London porter and Dublin stout mixed, half of each.

Ale Cup.

In a glass pitcher put the juice of half a lemon, one jigger of brandy, one heaping tablespoonful of fine sugar, one quart old ale; mix. When serving, grate a little nutmeg on top of each glass.

Badminton Cup.

Put a few lumps of ice into a glass pitcher, add two jiggers of sherry wine, one jigger maraschino, one tablespoonful fine sugar, one bottle claret, one slice of cucumber-rind, a few sprigs of borage, and a cold bottle of plain soda. Mix well and serve.

Balaklava Cup.

Cut the peel from a lemon in one long piece, put it with a few lumps of ice in a glass pitcher, add one tablespoonful fine sugar, the juice of the lemon, a slice of cucumber-rind, one pint claret; mix well, add a pint of cold champagne, and serve.

Cupid.

A mixing-glass half-full fine ice, one jigger sherry, one fresh egg, a little cayenne pepper. Shake well, strain, and serve.

Burgundy Cup (Red).

Mix one tablespoonful fine sugar with a little water in a glass pitcher, add the juice of half a lemon, one pony brandy, one pony orange curaçoa, a few lumps of ice, two slices lemon, two slices orange, one slice cucumber-peel, one pint red Burgundy, one bottle of cold plain soda; mix. Place a few sprigs of mint on top.

Burgundy Cup (White).

Mix in the same manner as Red Burgundy, substituting white Burgundy for red, and white curaçoa for orange.

Champagne Cup No. 1.

Put into a glass pitcher two or three lumps of clear ice, the juice of half a lemon, one-half tablespoonful fine sugar, one pony maraschino, one pony white curaçoa, one pony pale brandy, a few slices of orange, two slices of lemon, one slice cucumber-rind; pour in one quart of cold champagne, one bottle of cold plain soda; mix. Top off with a few sprigs of fresh mint.

Champagne Cup No. 2.

Three lumps of ice in a glass pitcher, add one tablespoonful fine sugar, one pony maraschino or white curaçoa, one pony pale brandy, one lemon sliced, one orange sliced, one slice cucumber-peel, pour in one pint claret, one quart iced champagne, one bottle cold plain soda. Mix and add a few sprigs fresh mint.

Cider Cup.

Put into a glass pitcher one tablespoonful fine sugar, a little water—dissolve; add the juice of half a lemon, a few lumps of clear ice, half a pony white curaçoa, half a pony brandy, one pint cider, one bottle plain soda, two slices of lemon, two of orange, one of cucumber-rind, a few lumps of clear ice; mix until cold. Add a few sprigs of fresh mint on top, stems down.

Claret Cup.

A heaping tablespoonful fine sugar, dissolve with a little water in a glass pitcher containing a few lumps of clear ice; add the juice of half a lemon, one pony brandy, half a pony maraschino, half a pony orange curaçoa, half an orange sliced, two slices of lemon, one slice cucumber-rind, one pint claret, one cold bottle plain soda; mix. Finish with a few sprigs of mint on top, stems down.

Claret Cup (per glass).

Dissolve in a long thin bar-glass one teaspoonful fine sugar, three dashes lemon-juice and two dashes orange curaçoa in a little water; add one lump of ice, two jiggers claret, one slice orange, one small piece of cucumber-rind. Mix and fill glass with seltzer.

Claret Cup à l'Anglaise.

This is a modification of the English claret cup, and shares the general fashionable rage for all things à l'Anglaise. Take twelve ounces of fine sugar, the zest of a lemon, two oranges without their seeds, pour upon this two bottles of claret and two bottles plain soda; add the small end of a cucumber not peeled (if you have borage add a little). Pour this mixture into a large bowl upon chopped ice. Serve when cold.

Claret Cup (English Style).

Put into a punch-bowl one large piece of clear ice, one tablespoonful fine sugar, one lemon sliced thin, one slice cucumber-rind, one pony curaçoa, one jigger sherry, one pint claret; add a little borage, a few strawberries, and one bottle plain soda. Stir until cold and serve.

Claret and Seltzer.

A long thin bar-glass half-full claret, then fill with cold seltzer.

Heidsieck Cup.

Mix same as Champagne Cup, using Heidsieck champagne.

India Cup (per glass).

One tablespoonful fine sugar, a little water, one slice lemon, two jiggers claret, one dash curaçoa, two dashes Madeira; mix well in thin punch-glass, add a slice cucumber, fill the glass with cold seltzer.

Lincoln Club Cup.

Put into a glass pitcher a few lumps of ice, one tablespoonful fine sugar, one jigger brandy, one jigger pale sherry, one jigger sauterne or rhine-wine, one lemon sliced, half an orange sliced, a few slices pineapple, one piece cucumber-rind, one iced bottle champagne, one bottle plain soda; mix. Serve cold.

Marmora Cup.

Three lumps of clear ice in a glass pitcher, the juice of half a lemon, one jigger orgeat syrup, half a pony brandy, half a pony maraschino, half a pony Jamaica rum, one tablespoonful fine sugar; add one iced bottle champagne, one bottle cold plain soda. Mix well, ornament with fruit in season, put a few sprigs fresh mint on top.

Royal Cup.

Dissolve two tablespoonfuls fine sugar with a little water in a punch-bowl, add the juice of one orange, the juice of half a lemon, one jigger brandy, one pony curaçoa, one pony maraschino, a few slices of pineapple, orange and lemon; pour on this one bottle of claret, then add three or four good-sized lumps of clear ice; mix well, and when cold add one bottle of plain soda and one bottle of iced champagne. Mix and serve.

Sauterne Cup.

Prepare same as Champagne Cup, substituting sauterne for champagne.

Brandy Daisy.

A mixing-glass half-full fine ice, three dashes gum-syrup, the juice of half a lemon, three dashes orange cordial, one jigger brandy; shake well, strain into fizz-glass, fill with siphon seltzer or apollinaris.

Gin Daisy.

Is prepared in the same manner as Brandy Daisy, using gin in place of brandy.

Ginger Ale Daisy.

Prepare same as Brandy Daisy, but strain into a long thin punch-glass and fill up with imported ginger ale in place of seltzer or apollinaris.

Rum Daisy.

Prepare same as Brandy Daisy, using rum in place of brandy.

Whiskey Daisy.

Prepare same as Brandy Daisy, using whiskey in place of brandy.

Baltimore Egg-Nogg.

The yolk of a fresh egg in a large mixing-glass, half a tablespoonful powdered sugar, a little grated nutmeg and cinnamon; beat until thoroughly mixed, add a few lumps of ice, one pony Madeira wine, half a pony old brandy, half a pony Jamaica rum, fill the glass with milk, shake well, strain into long thin punch-glass, a little grated nutmeg on top.

Boston Egg-Nogg.

A mixing-glass one-fourth full fine ice, one tablespoonful fine sugar, one egg, one-third jigger brandy, one-third jigger Jamaica rum, one-third Madeira wine; fill the glass with milk, shake well, strain into long thin punch-glass, a little grated nutmeg on top.

Cider Egg-Nogg.

One tablespoonful fine sugar, one egg in mixing-glass half-full fine ice; fill with cider; mix well, strain into long punch-glass, a little grated nutmeg on top. This drink is also known as General Harrison Egg-Nogg.

Plain Egg-Nogg.

One fresh egg, one tablespoonful fine sugar, half a jigger brandy, half a jigger St. Croix rum, in a mixing-glass one-fourth full of fine ice; fill with milk, shake well, strain into long thin glass, grate nutmeg on top.

Sherry Egg-Nogg.

A mixing-glass one-fourth full fine ice, one fresh egg, one jigger sherry, half a tablespoonful fine sugar; fill up with milk, shake thoroughly, strain into a long thin glass, grate nutmeg on top.

Sherry Egg-Nogg (Fancy).

Prepare in the same manner as Sherry Egg-Nogg, but add a pony of brandy before shaking.

Eye-Opener.

A mixing-glass half-full fine ice, half a tablespoonful fine sugar, juice of half a lime, one egg, one jigger old whiskey. Shake well, strain into a long thin bar-glass, fill with siphon vichy. Serve.

Mulled Ale (English Style).

For each glass take the yolk of one egg, half a tablespoonful fine sugar, and one tablespoonful cream or milk; beat until quite smooth. Heat your ale until quite hot, but not boiling; mix in the above preparation, stir well, and grate a little nutmeg on top.

Egg Phosphate.

A fresh egg in a mixing-glass half-full fine ice, add half a tablespoonful fine sugar and one teaspoonful of acid phosphate. Shake well, strain into a thin glass, fill up with siphon seltzer or vichy.

Egg-Shake.

One egg, one tablespoonful fine sugar in a mixing-glass half-full fine ice, fill with milk. Shake well and strain.

Egg Sour.

A mixing-glass half-full fine ice, the juice of half a lemon, one egg, one jigger of whiskey, half tablespoonful fine sugar. Shake well, strain into fancy glass. Serve.

Apple Brandy Fix.

A mixing-glass half-full fine ice, one tablespoonful fine sugar dissolved in a little water, half a pony curaçoa, one jigger apple brandy. Mix, serve in long thin glass with straws, trim with fruit; add a squirt of seltzer before serving.

Brandy Fix.

Prepare in the same manner as Apple Brandy Fix, substituting plain brandy for apple brandy.

Gin Fix.

One small spoonful fine sugar, one squirt of seltzer, half a pony pineapple syrup, one jigger gin in a long thin glass. Fill with fine ice, mix with spoon, trim with fruit. Serve with straws.

St. Croix Fix.

In a long thin glass, one tablespoonful fine sugar, half a pony pineapple syrup, three dashes lemon-juice, enough water to dissolve the above; add one jigger St. Croix rum. Fill glass with fine ice, mix, trim with fruit. Serve with straws.

Whiskey Fix.

Dissolve one tablespoonful sugar with a little water in a long thin glass, add five dashes pineapple syrup, the juice of a quarter of a lemon, one jigger whiskey. Fill the glass full of fine ice, mix well with spoon, trim with fruit. Serve in a long thin glass with straws.

Brandy Fizz.

A mixing-glass half full fine ice, the juice of half a lemon, half a tablespoonful fine sugar, one jigger brandy; shake well, strain into fizz-glass, fill with siphon seltzer. Serve.

Cider Fizz.

A thin fizz-glass two-thirds full cider; add the juice of quarter of a lemon, a long bar-spoonful fine sugar. Stir and drink during effervescence.

Gin Fizz.

Prepare in the same manner as Brandy Fizz, substituting gin for brandy.

Electric Current Fizz.

Make a silver fizz; save the yolk of the egg and serve it in the half-shell, with a little pepper, salt, and vinegar, with the fizz.

Golden Fizz.

The juice of half a lemon, half a tablespoonful fine sugar, the yolk of one egg, one jigger Tom gin; shake well in a mixing-glass with fine ice, strain into a fizz-glass, fill with siphon seltzer or carbonic. Drink while effervescent.

Lime Gin Fizz.

Prepare in the same manner as a Plain Gin Fizz, using lime-juice in place of lemon.

Morning Glory Fizz.

Fill a mixing-glass half-full fine ice; add the juice of half a lemon, half a tablespoonful fine sugar, the white of an egg, one jigger Scotch whiskey, two dashes absinthe; shake thoroughly, strain into a fizz-glass, fill with siphon seltzer. Serve.

New Orleans Fizz.

Half a tablespoonful fine sugar, the juice of half a small lemon, one jigger Tom gin; shake in a mixing-glass half-full fine ice, then add half a jigger milk or cream, shake again, strain into a fizz-glass, and fill with siphon seltzer or carbonic.

Pistache Fizz.

A mixing-glass one-fourth full fine ice, the juice of half a lemon, one-half tablespoonful fine sugar, one jigger Tom gin, one jigger full prepared pistache cream; shake well, strain into fizz-glass, fill with seltzer.

Royal Fizz.

Prepare same as Plain Gin Fizz, adding both the white and the yolk of a fresh egg before shaking; strain into fizz-glass and fill with siphon seltzer.

Sauterne Fizz.

One teaspoonful fine sugar in a long fizz-glass; add three dashes lemon-juice, one and a half jigger sauterne. Mix well and fill the glass with seltzer.

Silver Fizz.

A mixing-glass half-full fine ice, the juice of half a lemon, half a tablespoonful fine sugar, the white of one egg, one jigger Tom gin; shake well, strain into a fizz-glass, fill with siphon seltzer. Drink while effervescent.

Soda Fizz.

Mix the juice of one lemon with one tablespoonful fine sugar in a fizzglass, fill three-fourths full seltzer; add a small bar-spoonful bicarbonate of soda. Stir and drink during effervescence. This drink is a good stomach settler.

St. Croix Fizz.

A mixing-glass half-full fine ice, the juice of half a lemon, half a tablespoonful fine sugar, the white of an egg, one jigger St. Croix rum, shake well, strain into fizz-glass, fill with siphon seltzer.

Tailor's Fizz.

One lump of ice in a fizz-glass; add one jigger Scotch whiskey, fill the glass with siphon carbonic or vichy.

Violet Fizz.

Prepare in the same manner as a Silver Fizz, adding a tablespoonful raspberry vinegar before shaking.

Whiskey Fizz.

Prepare in the same manner as Brandy Fizz, substituting whiskey for brandy.

Ale Flip.

Beat up one egg with half a tablespoonful fine sugar, then fill the glass with ale; mix well with the egg and sugar. Grate nutmeg on top and serve.

Brandy Flip.

A mixing-glass half-full fine ice, one tablespoonful fine sugar, one fresh egg, one jigger brandy; shake well, strain into thin glass. Grate nutmeg on top.

Egg Flip.

One fresh egg, one tablespoonful fine sugar, one jigger sherry in a mixing-glass half-full fine ice;

shake well, strain into thin glass, grate nutmeg on top.

Gin Flip.

Prepare in the same manner as Egg Flip, substituting Tom gin for sherry.

Glasgow Flip.

Beat up a fresh egg with one tablespoonful fine sugar and the juice of one lemon. Put this preparation in a long thin glass, add a lump of ice, fill up with a cold bottle of imported ginger ale; mix well. Serve.

Golden Flip.

One pony maraschino, one pony yellow chartreuse, half a tablespoonful fine sugar, one egg; shake well in a mixing-glass half-full fine ice, strain into a fancy bar-glass, grate a little nutmeg on top.

Jamaica Rum Flip.

Fill a mixing-glass half-full fine ice, add half a tablespoonful fine sugar, one egg, one jigger Jamaica rum; shake well, strain into a fancy bar-glass. Serve with a little grated nutmeg on top.

Port Wine Flip.

Prepare in the same manner as Jamaica Rum Flip, substituting port wine for rum.

Rum Flip.

Prepare same as Sherry Flip, using the kind of rum desired by the customer in place of sherry.

Sherry Flip.

Break a fresh egg into a mixing-glass; add one tablespoonful fine sugar, fill the glass half-full of fine ice, add one and a half jigger of sherry; shake well, strain into a fancy bar-glass. Serve with a little grated nutmeg on top.

Whiskey Flip.

Prepare in the same manner as Sherry Flip, substituting whiskey for sherry.

Yankee Flip.

Prepare in the same manner as Sherry Flip, using one jigger apple brandy in place of sherry.

Floster.

Place a few lumps of ice in a glass pitcher, add half a tablespoonful fine sugar, two jiggers sherry, one jigger noyau, a few slices of lemon and orange, one bottle plain soda; mix. Put a few sprigs fresh mint on top.

Brandy Float.

Fill a pony-glass with brandy, put a thin whiskey-glass over it, rim down; reverse the glasses, holding them tightly together, so as to keep the brandy in the pony glass, then fill the whiskey-glass half-full seltzer and draw out the pony glass carefully so as to leave the brandy floating on top of seltzer.

Curaçoa Float.

Fill a pony-glass half-full maraschino, then fill with orange curaçoa, be careful to keep the two cordials in separate layers.

Absinthe Frappé, No. 1.

Take two mixing-glasses and fill them full of fine ice, pour into one of them one pony absinthe, one pony water, add two dashes anisette. Turn the other mixing-glass full of fine ice on top of first glass, then reverse the glasses, so as to allow the liquid to flow from one glass to the other. Repeat this until the liquid is very cold, then strain into a fancy bar-glass and add a squirt of seltzer.

Absinthe Frappé, No. 2.

A mixing-glass half-full fine ice; add one pony of absinthe, one pony of water, one dash anisette; shake until ice forms on outside of shaker, strain into thin glass, add a squirt of seltzer.

Brandy Punch Frappé.

Fill two mixing-glasses with fine ice; put into one of them one tablespoonful fine sugar, a little water, the juice of half a lemon, one jigger brandy. Turn the second glass on top of first; leave there a moment, then turn the glasses so as to allow the liquid to flow from one glass into the other. Repeat this until the mixture is very cold; strain into a fancy glass, trim with fruits in season.

Coffee Frappé.

Dissolve one lump of sugar with one demi-tasse of cold coffee in a mixing-glass; add a few lumps of ice, one pony brandy. Shake well and strain into a fancy bar-glass.

Brandy Frappé.

Take two mixing-glasses of the same size, fill them with fine shaven ice; pour into one of them one jigger brandy and a few dashes maraschino. Turn the second glass on top of first, then reverse the glasses several times, holding them together so as to allow the liquid to slowly flow from one glass to the other; when cold strain into fancy glass.

Cordial Frappé.

Fill a fancy sauterne or claret glass with fine ice, add a pony of the kind of cordial desired by the customer. Let it stand until ice forms on the outside of the glass, then serve.

Raspberry Cream Frappé.

This delicious temperance drink is made in the following manner: Fill a long thin punch-glass half-full fine ice, add one jigger raspberry syrup, fill up the glass two-thirds with cream or milk, then fill with siphon vichy; mix. Trim with fruit. Serve with straws.

French Vermouth Frappé.

Fill two mixing-glasses with fine ice; pour into one of them one jigger French vermouth. Turn the second glass on top of the first, reverse the glasses so as to allow the liquid to flow from one glass to the other, repeat this until the mixture is very cold, strain into a thin glass, add a squirt of seltzer.

Italian Vermouth Frappé.

Prepare in the same manner as French Vermouth Frappé, using Italian vermouth in place of French.

Whiskey Punch Frappé.

Prepare same as Brandy Punch Frappé, using whiskey in place of brandy.

French Café Royal.

Three ponies black coffee, one pony brandy, make very cold. Serve after dinner.

Gin and Pine.

Take from the heart of a green pine log two ounces of splinters, steep in a quart bottle Tom gin for twenty-four hours, strain into another bottle. Serve same as straight gin.

Gin and Tansy.

Steep a bunch of tansy in a bottle of gin until the flavor is extracted, then strain into another bottle. Serve same as gin and pine.

Gin and Wormwood.

Steep a small bunch of wormwood in one quart of gin until the flavor is extracted. Serve same as Gin and Tansy.

Golden Slipper.

Fill a wine-glass one-third full of yellow chartreuse, add the yolk of a small egg, then fill the glass with Danziger Goldwasser; be careful not to break the yolk of the egg, and keep the cordials separate.

Grenadine Lemonade.

Make a plain lemonade rather tart, and add a pony of grenadine before shaking. Trim with fruit, serve with straws.

Half and Half (American Style).

A glass half-full of old ale, fill up with new ale.

Half and Half (English Style).

A glass or mug half-full porter, then fill up with ale.

Hari-Kari.

A mixing-glass half-full fine ice, one tablespoonful fine sugar, the juice of half a lemon, one jigger Bourbon whiskey; shake well, strain into a long thin glass, fill with seltzer. Trim with fruit.

Horse's Neck.

Cut the peel from a lemon in one long piece, place in a thin punch-glass, add a bottle of cold imported ginger ale.

Hot Apple Toddy.

One lump sugar dissolved with a little water in a hot-drink glass, add one jigger apple brandy, a piece lemon peel, a quarter of a baked apple, fill with boiling water; mix, and grate nutmeg on top.

Hot Arrack Punch.

Two lumps of sugar in a hot-drink glass half-full boiling water, the juice of one-fourth of a lemon, one jigger arrack, one slice lemon; mix and grate a little nutmeg on top.

Hot Beef-Tea.

A small teaspoonful extract of beef in a hot-drink glass, or mug, fill with boiling water, season to taste with pepper and salt, add two dashes celery bitters; mix, and serve with a small glass of fine ice on the side.

Hot Black Stripe.

A hot-drink glass half-full boiling water, one jigger of rum, a small spoonful molasses; mix well and add a small piece lemon-peel.

Hot Brandy Punch.

Prepare same as hot Arrack Punch, substituting brandy for arrack; leave out the nutmeg.

Hot Brandy Sling.

Dissolve a lump of cut-loaf sugar in a hot-drink glass half-full of boiling water, add one jigger of brandy; mix, add a piece of lemon peel, grate a little nutmeg on top.

Hot Brandy Toddy.

Prepare same as Hot Brandy Sling without nutmeg.

Hot Cider Punch.

Put three lumps of sugar, the juice of one-fourth of a lemon, and three cloves in a hot-drink glass, fill up with hot cider; mix, add a slice of lemon and a little grated nutmeg.

Hot Gin Punch.

Prepare same as Hot Brandy Punch, using gin in place of brandy.

Hot Gin Sling.

Prepare in the same manner as Hot Brandy Sling, substituting gin for brandy.

Hot Spiced Gin.

Prepare same as Hot Gin Sling, adding a few cloves and a little ground allspice.

Hot Irish Punch.

A hot-drink glass half full-boiling water, two lumps of cut-loaf sugar, the juice of a quarter of a lemon, one jigger of Irish whiskey; mix, and add a slice of lemon and a little grated nutmeg.

Hot Irish Sling.

Prepare same as Hot Irish Punch, leaving out the lemon.

Classic Cocktail Guides and Retro Bartender Books

Hot Jamaica Rum Punch.

One lump of sugar in a hot-drink glass, add a little lemon-juice, one slice lemon, one jigger of Jamaica rum, fill up with boiling water; mix, grate a little nutmeg on top.

Hot Jamaica Rum Sling.

Prepare same as Hot Jamaica Rum Punch, but leave out the lemon-juice and sliced lemon, add a piece lemon-peel.

Hot Jamaica Rum Spiced.

A hot-drink glass half full of boiling water, one lump of sugar, one jigger Jamaica rum, a few cloves and a little allspice; mix, add a small piece of lemon-peel and a little grated nutmeg on top.

Hot Kentucky Flip.

Beat up one egg with a pinch of ground cloves, the same of cinnamon, the juice of a quarter of a lemon, half a tablespoonful fine sugar, one jigger Jamaica rum; when well mixed divide into two hot-drink glasses, fill with boiling water; stir and serve.

Hot Lemonade.

The juice of half a lemon, one-half tablespoonful fine sugar, fill up with hot water; mix, add a slice of lemon.

Hot Locomotive.

Beat up the yolk of one egg in a small saucepan with one tablespoonful fine sugar, one pony of honey, four dashes orange curaçoa, one and a half jiggers claret. Put on fire, let it come to the boiling point; mix well. Serve in a mug, add a slice of lemon.

Hot Milk Punch.

Put into a long thin punch-glass one tablespoonful fine sugar, half a jigger brandy, half a jigger St. Croix rum, fill with hot milk; mix and grate a little nutmeg on top.

Hot Scotch.

Dissolve one lump of cut-loaf sugar with a little hot water in a hot-drink glass, add one jigger Scotch whiskey and a small piece lemon-peel, fill with boiling water; mix, grate a little nutmeg on top.

Hot Scotch Punch.

Prepare same as Hot Brandy Punch, substituting Scotch whiskey for brandy.

Hot Whiskey Sling.

One lump of sugar in a hot-drink glass half-full boiling water, add one jigger of whiskey, a small piece lemon-peel; mix and grate a little nutmeg on top.

Classic Cocktail Guides and Retro Bartender Books

Hot Whiskey Punch.

Prepare in the same manner as Hot Whiskey Sling, adding a slice of lemon and the juice of a quarter of a lemon before mixing; leave the nutmeg out.

Brandy Julep.

Half a tablespoonful fine sugar dissolved with a little water in a long thin glass, add a few sprigs of fresh mint, stems down, fill with fine ice, add one jigger brandy; mix well with bar-spoon, trim with fruit and a few sprigs of mint. Serve with straws.

Champagne Julep.

Dissolve one lump of sugar with a little water in a long thin glass, add a few sprigs of fresh mint, stems down, fill the glass almost full of fine ice, then fill with champagne, stirring with spoon while pouring in the wine; trim with fruit and sprigs of mint. Serve straws.

Gin Julep.

One small lump of sugar dissolved with a little water in a long thin glass, a few sprigs of mint, stems down, fill with fine ice, add one jigger of gin; mix, trim with fruit and sprigs of mint. Serve with straws.

Mint Julep (Southern Style).

Half a tablespoonful fine sugar dissolved in a long thin glass with a little water, add a few sprigs of mint, stems down, fill the glass with fine ice, add half a jigger of brandy, half jigger rum; mix well, trim with fruit and sprigs of mint. Serve straws.

Whiskey Julep.

Prepare in the same manner as Brandy Julep, using whiskey in place of brandy.

Knickerbein.

A wineglass one-third full of vanilla cordial, the yolk of one egg, cover the egg carefully with benedictine, fill the glass with kümmel, add two drops of Angostura bitters. See that the different ingredients are not mixed.

Knickerbocker.

Put into a long glass the juice of half a lemon, one pony raspberry syrup, half a pony curaçoa, one jigger St. Croix rum, fill the glass with fine ice; mix well, trim with a slice of pineapple, orange and lemon. Serve with straws.

Lalla Rookh.

A mixing-glass half-full fine ice, add one pony vanilla cordial, one-half jigger brandy, half a jigger rum, a small spoonful fine sugar, a whiskey-glass full cream; shake well, strain into a long thin bar-glass.

Angostura Lemonade.

The juice of one lemon, one tablespoonful fine sugar in a mixing-glass half-full fine ice, add three dashes Angostura bitters, fill up with water; shake well, put in long thin glass, trim with fruits in season. Serve on ice with straws or strain, as desired.

Lemon Squash.

Cut a whole lemon into halves, place them in a mixing-glass, add one tablespoonful of powdered sugar, crush the lemon with muddler to extract the juice, fill the glass half-full fine ice, add a cold bottle of plain soda, mix with spoon; put all into a long thin punch-glass, ornament with fruits in season, and serve with straws.

Lemon Syrup.

Take one gallon gum-syrup, add to it three pints of pure lemon juice, put on the fire and bring to the boiling-point; when cold bottle, cork, and keep in a cool place.

Egg Lemonade.

A mixing-glass half-full fine ice, the juice of half a lemon, one tablespoonful fine sugar, one egg, fill with water; shake well, and strain, or leave on ice and serve with straws.

Phosphate Lemonade.

One tablespoonful fine sugar, one tablespoonful acid phosphate in a mixing-glass; fill half-full fine ice, fill with water; shake well, trim with fruit in season. Serve straws or strain.

Plain Lemonade.

The juice of one lemon in a mixing-glass half full fine ice, add one tablespoonful fine sugar, fill with water; shake well, trim with fruit and serve with straws, or strain to suit customer.

Rhine-Wine Lemonade.

Make a plain lemonade, strain it into a long thin glass, trim with fruit, top it off with a jigger of Rhine-wine.

Seltzer Lemonade.

Prepare same as Plain Lemonade, using seltzer in place of water; mix with long bar-spoon.

Soda Lemonade.

Prepare same as Seltzer Lemonade; use a bottle of plain soda in place of seltzer.

Tea Lemonade.

Prepare in the same manner as a Plain Lemonade, using cold tea in the place of water.

Limeade.

Mix same as Plain Lemonade, using the juice of limes in place of lemon.

Italian Wine Lemonade.

Dissolve one tablespoonful fine sugar with a little water in a long thin punch-glass, add half a pony raspberry syrup, the juice of the quarter of an orange, the same of lemon, one jigger dry sherry, fill the glass three-fourths full fine ice, then fill with cold water; mix well, ornament with fruit in season. Serve straws.

White Lion.

Cut the peel of half a lemon from it in one long thin piece, place it in a mixing-glass, add the juice of half a lemon, one tablespoonful fine sugar, one tablespoonful raspberry syrup, one jigger St. Croix rum, one pony curaçoa; mix well, put all in a long thin glass, ornament with fruit. Serve straws.

Alderman's Nip.

A small lump of ice in a whiskey-glass, one dash acid phosphate, a small piece lemon-peel, one dash Peyschaud bitters, two dashes gum-syrup, one jigger whiskey; serve with a small bar-spoon in the glass.

Cider Nectar.

A long thin glass half-full fine ice, one and a half jiggers cider, half a jigger brandy, half a jigger sherry, a tablespoonful gum-syrup; mix well with spoon, fill with seltzer, trim with fruit. Sip with straws.

Port Wine Negus.

This is simply a hot port. Take one lump of sugar in a hot-drink glass, add one jigger port wine, fill with hot water; mix, grate nutmeg on top.

Sherry Wine Negus.

Prepare same as Port Wine Negus, using sherry in place of port wine.

Orangeade.

The juice of half a juicy orange, the juice of a quarter of a lemon, half a tablespoonful fine sugar; put in a mixing-glass, fill half-full fine ice, fill with cold water. Mix well, serve with straws in a long thin glass, trim with fruit.

Café Parfait.

Three lumps of ice in a mixing-glass, add one jigger strong coffee, three jiggers pure cream, half a teaspoonful fine sugar; shake until cold, strain into long thin glass.

Pousse Cafe (American Style).

Fill a thin cordial-glass with one-fourth maraschino, one-fourth orange curaçoa, one-fourth green chartreuse, and one-fourth brandy. Be careful to have the cordials in separate layers.

Pousse Cafe (French Style).

Fill a pousse-café glass one-fifth full grenadine, one-fifth maraschino, one-fifth orange curaçoa, one-fifth green chartreuse, one-fifth cognac; keep liqueurs in separate layers.

Pousse Cafe (Jersey Lily).

A pony-glass half-full maraschino, fill up with brandy, add five drops Angostura bitters. Be careful to keep colors separate.

Pousse Cafe (New Orleans Style).

A sherry wineglass one-fifth full maraschino, one-fifth raspberry syrup, one-fifth orange curaçoa, one-fifth green chartreuse, one-fifth brandy. Ignite the brandy, let it burn a few moments, extinguish, and serve.

Pousse d'Amour.

A sherry-glass one-third full of maraschino, carefully add the yolk of a fresh egg, fill the glass with yellow chartreuse; keep the two liqueurs in separate layers.

Peach and Honey.

Pour a little peach brandy into a small bar-glass, add a teaspoonful honey; mix well. Place peach brandy before customer and allow him to help himself.

Peach Blow.

Crush six ripe strawberries with half a tablespoonful fine sugar in a mixing-glass, fill glass one-third full fine ice, add one jigger brandy, fill up with milk; shake well, strain.

Pick Me Up.

A mixing-glass half full fine ice, half a pony absinthe, one jigger vermouth; shake well until cold, strain into a star-glass, fill with seltzer.

Apple Brandy Punch.

Fill a mixing-glass three-fourths full of fine ice, add the juice of half a lemon, one tablespoonful fine sugar, one jigger apple brandy; shake well. Serve on ice with straws or strain, trim with fruit.

Arrack Punch.

Squeeze the juice of half a lemon into a mixing-glass half-full of fine ice, add one tablespoonful fine sugar, one jigger arrack; shake well, and serve same as Apple Brandy Punch.

Boating Club Punch.

In a mixing-glass the juice of one lime, one tablespoonful fine sugar, add a little water, fill glass half-full fine ice, add one-half jigger brandy, half jigger St. Croix rum; shake well, serve on ice in a long thin glass, ornament with fruits in season. Serve straws.

Hot Boland Punch.

A hot-drink glass one-third full boiling water, add one lump of sugar, one jigger Scotch whiskey, fill up with ginger ale, add a piece twisted lemon peel, grate nutmeg on top.

Bonanza Punch (For a Party).

Five quarts cold water, four and one-half pounds of fine sugar, the juice of twelve lemons, three oranges, one can pineapple, one-half pint Tom gin, one pint white wine. Grate the rinds of three lemons and two oranges into a bowl, add the juice of the oranges and lemons.

Put two quarts water, two pounds sugar, and

the juice of pineapple on the fire, make a hot syrup of this, then pour it on the grated rinds and the juice to draw the flavor; chop the pineapple fine and add to mixture; stir well and strain all into a large punch-bowl half-full of very fine ice, add remainder of sugar and water, the gin, and wine; mix until cold, trim with fruit. Serve on ice with straws.

Brandy Punch.

A mixing-glass half-full fine ice, add one tablespoonful fine sugar, the juice of half a lemon, one jigger brandy; shake well, serve on ice in long thin glass, trim with fruit. Serve with straws.

Brandy Punch (Strained).

Prepare in the same manner as Brandy Punch, strain into fancy glass, ornament with fruit. Serve.

Brandy Milk Punch.

A large mixing-glass one-third full fine ice, half a tablespoonful fine sugar, one jigger brandy, fill with cold milk; shake well, strain into a long thin punch-glass, grate a little nutmeg on top. Serve straws.

Canadian Club Punch.

One tablespoonful fine sugar dissolved in a little water in mixing-glass, fill half-full fine ice, add the juice of half a lemon, one jigger Walker Canadian whiskey; shake well, strain into fancy glass, top off with a little claret, trim with fruit.

Century Club Punch.

Fill a mixing-glass half-full fine ice, add one tablespoonful fine sugar, a little water, the juice of half a lemon, half a jigger Jamaica rum, half a jigger St. Croix rum; shake well. Serve in a long thin glass with straws, trim with fruits in season.

Champagne Punch.

Dissolve one tablespoonful fine sugar with a little water in a glass pitcher or a punch-bowl, add a few lumps of clear ice, the juice of half a lemon, a few slices orange and pineapple, one bottle plain soda; mix well, add one pint champagne. Stir well and serve.

Fancy Champagne Punch.

Put into a glass pitcher or a punch-bowl a few lumps clear ice, six lumps of domino sugar, one pint Burgundy, one orange cut in thin slices, one half lemon sliced, one pony brandy, one pony maraschino, one pint cold apollinaris, one pint cold champagne; mix well. Serve in punch-glasses.

Chocolate Punch.

A mixing-glass half-full fine ice, add one tablespoonful fine sugar, one egg, one-half jigger port wine, one-half jigger brandy, the juice of half a lemon; shake well, strain into fancy glass.

Cider Punch.

Dissolve one tablespoonful fine sugar with a little water and the juice of a quarter of a lemon in a mixing-glass, fill half-full with fine ice, add one pony brandy, fill up with cider; mix well. Serve on ice, with straws, trim with fruit in season.

Claret Punch.

Dissolve one and a half tablepoonsfuls fine sugar with one jigger water in a large mixing-glass, add the juice of a quarter of a lemon, two jiggers claret, fill the glass with fine ice; shake well, serve in a long thin punch-glass, leave on ice or strain, trim with fruit. If on ice serve straws.

Club Punch.

One tablespoonful fine sugar dissolved in a little water in a mixing-glass, fill glass half full fine ice, add the juice of half a lemon, one-third jigger Jamaica rum, two-thirds jigger St. Croix rum; mix well, strain into a fancy glass, trim with fruit, top off with a little port wine.

Cosmopolitan Punch.

Mix same as Claret Punch, adding a pony brandy before shaking.

Curaçoa Punch.

One-half tablespoonful fine sugar, the juice of half a lemon, one pony curaçoa, one pony brandy in mixing-glass, fill with fine ice; shake well. Put into long thin glass, add a dash of Jamaica rum, trim with fruit. Serve straws.

Domino Punch.

Dissolve a tablespoonful fine sugar with a little water and the juice of half a lemon, add one pony of port wine, one pony brandy, a dash of maraschino. Put all in mixing-glass, fill with fine ice; shake well, strain into a fancy glass, ornament with choice fruit.

Fedora Punch.

A tablespoonful fine sugar dissolved in a mixing-glass with a little water, add the juice of half a lemon, one pony brandy, one pony Bourbon whiskey, half a pony curaçoa, half a pony Jamaica rum, fill the glass with fine ice; shake well. Serve in a long thin punch-glass, trim with fruit. Sip with straws.

Fish House Punch.

Fill a mixing-glass half-full fine ice, add the juice of half a lemon, one tablespoonful fine sugar, half a jigger brandy, half a pony Jamaica rum, half a pony peach brandy; shake well, strain into thin punch-glass.

Gin Punch.

A mixing-glass half-full fine ice, half a tablespoonful fine sugar, the juice of half a lemon, one jigger gin; shake well. Serve on ice with straws or strain, trim with fruit.

Gin Puff.

A mixing-glass half-full fine ice, add one jigger Tom gin, two jiggers milk; shake well, strain into a medium-sized glass and fill with siphon seltzer.

Gin Milk Punch.

Put into a large mixing-glass one tablespoonful fine sugar, add one jigger Tom gin, fill the glass one-third full fine ice, fill up with milk; shake well, strain into a long punch-glass, grate a little nutmeg on top. Serve.

Gin Tea Punch.

Grate off the yellow part of the rinds of six lemons into a punch-bowl, add one pound cut-loaf sugar, the juice of the six lemons, half a pint of boiling water; mix well, add two quarts old Tom gin. Infuse one teaspoonful coriander seeds in a pint of boiling green tea for twenty minutes, then add while hot to the mixture in the bowl, stir well and when cold strain, bottle, cork and seal. Keep in a cool place.

Glee Club Punch.

Put two lumps of sugar into a hot-drink glass, add a little lemon juice, three cloves, one small piece cinnamon, fill the glass half-full of boiling water, add one dash brandy, fill up with warm claret; mix well, grate a little nutmeg on top.

Hancock Punch.

Fill a mixing-glass half-full of fine ice, add the juice and rind of half a lime, half a tablespoonful fine sugar, one-third of a jigger St. Croix rum, two-thirds of a jigger whiskey; shake well, strain into long thin eight-ounce glass, fizz up with a little siphon seltzer.

Horsford Punch.

Dissolve half a tablespoonful fine sugar with a little water in a mixing-glass, add one teaspoonful Horsford's Acid Phosphate, one jigger brandy; shake well, strain into fancy glass, trim with fruit.

Imperial Punch.

Dissolve one tablespoonful fine sugar in a mixing glass with a little water, add two jiggers claret, half a pony of maraschino, a little grated nutmeg, two thin slices lemon, fill the glass with fine ice, add a squirt of seltzer; mix well, trim with fruit. Serve straws.

Irish Punch.

Fill a mixing-glass half-full of fine ice, add one tablespoonful fine sugar, a little water, the juice of half a lemon, one jigger Irish whiskey; mix well, strain into a fancy bar-glass, trim with fruit, or leave on ice, and serve with straws.

Jamaica Rum Punch.

Prepare in the same manner as Irish Punch, substituting Jamaica rum for Irish whiskey.

Japanese Punch.

One lump cut-loaf sugar dissolved with a little hot water in a hot-drink glass, add the juice of half a lime, half a jigger arrack, half a jigger brandy, fill the glass with hot tea; mix and serve. This punch is usually served with cake.

Fancy Kirsch Punch (For a Party).

Mix two quarts of water with two pounds of fine sugar, the juice of four lemons and one pint Kirschwasser. When the sugar is dissolved, strain the mixture into a punch-bowl containing a large lump of ice, stir until cold; then beat the whites of four eggs firm, add to the punch, sprinkle a little cinnamon on top.

Kirschwasser Punch.

Dissolve one tablespoonful fine sugar with a little water in a mixing-glass, add the juice of half a lemon, half a pony maraschino, one jigger Kirschwasser, fill the glass with fine ice. Mix well, trim with fruit. Sip with straws.

Knickerbocker Punch.

Fill a mixing-glass half-full fine ice, add half a tablespoonful fine sugar, three dashes pineapple syrup, three dashes curaçoa, the juice of half a lemon, one jigger St. Croix rum; mix well, strain into a fancy bar-glass, trim with fruit.

Manhattan Punch.

The juice of half a lemon in a mixing-glass, add half a tablespoonful fine sugar, two dashes Angostura bitters, one-half jigger whiskey, one-half jigger French vermouth; shake well, serve on ice in long glass, trim with fruit. Sip with straws.

Medford Rum Punch.

Dissolve a tablespoonful fine sugar with a little water in a mixing-glass, add the juice of half a lemon, fill the glass half-full fine ice, add one jigger Medford rum; mix well, strain into fancy bar-glass, and trim with fruit, or leave on ice and serve straws.

Mikado Punch.

Put into a mixing-glass one tablespoonful fine sugar, dissolve it with a little water, fill the glass half-full fine ice, add the juice of half a lemon, half a jigger brandy, half a jigger St. Croix rum; shake well, strain into a fancy bar-glass and ornament with fruit, or leave on ice and serve straws.

Milk Punch.

Fill a large mixing-glass one-third full of fine ice, add one tablespoonful fine sugar, half a jigger brandy, half a jigger St. Croix rum, fill up with milk; shake well, strain into a long thin punch-glass, and grate a little nutmeg on top.

Mississippi Punch.

In a mixing-glass one tablespoonful fine sugar, dissolve in a little water, add juice of half a lemon, half a jigger Bourbon whiskey, half a jigger Jamaica rum, one jigger brandy, fill the glass with fine ice; shake well, put in long thin punch-glass, ornament top with fruit. Serve straws.

National Punch.

Fill a mixing-glass half-full of fine ice, add the juice of half a lemon, one tablespoonful of fine sugar, half a jigger brandy, one jigger Rhine-wine; mix well. Serve on ice in a long punch-glass, ornament with fruit, float a little Jamaica rum on top. Serve straws.

Orange Punch.

Dissolve one tablespoonful fine sugar with a little water in a mixing-glass, add the juice of half an orange, the juice of half a lime, one jigger eau de vie d'oranges or orange brandy, fill the glass with fine ice; mix well; strain into fancy bar-glass, trim with fruit.

Orgeat Punch.

In a mixing-glass the juice of half a lemon, one jigger orgeat syrup, one jigger whiskey, fill the glass with fine ice; shake well, put all into a long thin punch-glass, trim with fruit, top off with claret. Serve with straws.

Peach Punch.

Put into a mixing-glass half a peach, either fresh or canned, one tablespoonful fine sugar, the juice of one-fourth of a lemon, one jigger brandy, fill with fine ice; mix well. Serve in the ice or strain into a fancy bar-glass.

Poland Punch.

Squeeze the juice of half a lemon into a mixing glass, add one tablespoonful fine sugar, one jigger whiskey, fill the glass with fine ice; shake well; strain into a long thin glass, fill up with cold Poland water.

Port Wine Punch.

The juice of half a lemon, half a tablespoonful fine sugar, one jigger port wine in a mixing-glass, fill up with fine ice; mix well. Serve in ice with straws, or strain into fancy glass, trim with fruit.

Presidential Punch.

Beat up the yolks of two eggs with two tablespoonfuls fine sugar, add two jiggers of orange brandy and the juice of half a lemon; mix well; divide into two hot-drink tumblers, fill with hot water, stir well, grate nutmeg on top. Serve.

Rebb. Davis Punch.

Crush half a lemon in a Briggs House glass, add one tablespoonful fine sugar, one lump ice, one jigger whiskey; mix well, trim with fruit, add a squirt of seltzer. Serve.

Rhine-Wine Punch.

A mixing-glass half-full fine ice, one tablespoonful fine sugar, the juice of one-fourth a lemon, two jiggers Rhine-wine; mix well, fill with siphon seltzer, trim with fruit. Serve straws.

Roman Punch.

Fill a large mixing-glass half-full of fine ice, add the juice of half an orange, the juice of half a lemon, one tablespoonful fine sugar, a little water to dissolve the sugar, half a jigger Jamaica rum, half a jigger brandy; mix well, trim with fruit. Serve on ice with straws.

Ruby Punch.

Dissolve half a tablespoonful fine sugar with a little water in a mixing-glass, fill the glass half full fine ice, add the juice of half a lemon, half a jigger port wine, half a jigger arrack, fill up with cold tea; mix well, trim with fruit. Serve straws.

Russian Punch.

The juice of half a lemon, one tablespooonful fine sugar in a mixing-glass half-full fine ice, add half a jigger allash, half a jigger orange brandy; mix well; strain into fancy bar-glass, trim with fruit.

Russian Tea Punch.

Dissolve one pound of cut-loaf sugar in three pints of hot green tea, add the juice of three lemons and three jiggers of crême d'allash, a few thin slices of lemon, serve hot, or when cold ice well and sip with straws.

Sauterne Punch.

In a mixing-glass, dissolve one tablespoonful fine sugar in a little water, add three slices of lemon, one and a half jiggers sauterne, fill the glass with fine ice; mix well. Put all into a long thin punch-glass, trim with fruit. Serve straws.

Scotch Whiskey Punch.

Prepare in the same manner as Brandy Punch, substituting Scotch whiskey for brandy.

Sherry Punch.

A mixing-glass half-full fine ice, half a tablespoonful fine sugar, the juice of one-fourth a lemon, the juice of one-fourth an orange, one and a half jiggers sherry; mix well, trim with fruit. Serve straws.

Siberian Punch.

The juice of half a lemon, one jigger water, and one tablespoonful fine sugar, dissolved in a mixing-glass, add one jigger Czarowitch (eau de vie d'oranges), fill the glass with fine ice; shake until very cold. Serve in a long thin glass, ornament with fruit. Sip with straws.

St. Charles Punch.

In a mixing-glass one teaspoonful fine sugar dissolved in a little water, add the juice of half a lemon, one jigger port wine, one pony brandy, a few dashes curaçoa, fill the glass with fine ice; mix well. Put all in a long thin glass, trim with fruit. Serve straws.

St. Croix Rum Punch.

One tablespoonful fine sugar dissolved with a little water in a mixing-glass, add the juice of half a lemon, one jigger of St. Croix rum, fill the glass with fine ice; mix well. Serve on ice with straws or strain, trim with fruit.

Steinway Punch.

Make a plain whiskey punch, strain into a long thin glass, and fill up with cold apollinaris water.

Tip Top Punch.

Put four lumps ice in a long thin glass, add one lump sugar, two slices lemon, one slice orange, one slice pineapple, one pony brandy, fill the glass with cold champagne, stir with long bar-spoon. Sip with straws.

Vanilla Punch.

Dissolve one tablespoonful fine sugar, with a little water in a mixing-glass, add the juice of half a small lemon, two dashes curaçoa, one jigger cognac, half a jigger vanilla cordial; mix well. Serve in long thin punch-glass, ornament with fruit. Serve straws.

West Indian Punch.

One lump of sugar dissolved in a little water in a mixing-glass, add the juice of half a lime, half a pony brandy, one jigger old Madeira, fill the glass with cracked ice; mix until cold, strain into fancy glass, decorate with berries and sliced fruit.

Whiskey Punch (Plain).

Fill a mixing-glass half-full fine ice, add one tablespoonful fine sugar, the juice of half a lemon, one jigger whiskey; mix well. Serve in long thin glass, trim with fruit. Sip with straws.

Whiskey Punch (Strained).

Prepare same as Plain Whiskey Punch, but strain into a fancy bar-glass before trimming with fruit.

Yale Punch.

In a punch-bowl containing a few large lumps of clear ice put four lumps of sugar, the juice of half a lemon, and one-half pint of red Burgundy to every quart of cold dry champagne; mix well, ornament with fruit. Pour champagne in last.

Brandy Rickey.

In a thin medium-sized glass put one lump of ice, the juice of half a lime, one jigger brandy, fill the glass with siphon carbonic water; drink while effervescent.

Canadian Rickey.

Is prepared in the same manner as Brandy Rickey, substituting Canadian Club whiskey for brandy.

Gin Rickey.

Prepare same as Brandy Rickey, substituting gin for brandy.

Reviver.

A sherry-glass one-third full maraschino, one-third noyau, and one-third yellow chartreuse.

Rhine-Wine and Seltzer.

Fill a thin glass half full of Rhine-wine, then fill up with seltzer. This is a favorite summer drink.

Rock and Rye.

Pour into a whiskey-glass one teaspoonful pure rock-candy syrup, add a small bar-spoon, and allow the customer to help himself to the whiskey.

Rum and Gum.

Place before the customer a whiskey-glass containing one teaspoonful gum syrup, and a small bar-spoon, then hand out the desired kind of rum and allow him to help himself.

Rum and Sugar.

Serve in the same manner as Rum and Gum, substituting a lump of sugar dissolved in a little water for gum.

Scotch Whiskey Rickey.

Concoct in the same manner as Brandy Rickey, substituting Scotch whiskey for brandy.

Vermouth Rickey.

Place one lump of ice in a medium-sized bar-glass, add the juice of half a lime, one jigger vermouth; stir with spoon, fill up with carbonic water, drink during effervescence.

Whiskey Rickey.

Prepare in the same manner as Vermouth Rickey, substituting whiskey for vermouth.

Ale Sangaree.

Dissolve a bar-spoonful of fine sugar in a glass of ale, mix well, and grate a little nutmeg on top.

Brandy Sangaree.

Fill a mixing-glass half-full of fine ice, add half a tablespoonful of fine sugar, one jigger brandy; shake well and strain, grate nutmeg on top.

Gin Sangaree.

Prepare same as Brandy Sangaree, using gin in place of brandy.

Port Wine Sangaree.

Prepare same as Brandy Sangaree, substituting port wine for brandy.

Sherry Sangaree.

Same as Port Wine Sangaree, using sherry wine in place of port.

Sam Ward.

This delicious after-dinner drink can be made either from yellow chartreuse or maraschino. Fill a claret-glass with very fine shaved ice, remove the rind from a slice of lemon, fit it on the inside of the rim of the glass; place a small piece twisted lemon-peel in the centre and fill up with the desired liqueur.

Schickler.

Pour into a long thin punch-glass one pony of brandy, one pony of grenadine, add one lump of ice, one bottle of cold plain soda; mix with long bar-spoon. Drink during effervescence.

Brandy Scaffa.

Pour into a cordial-glass one-third maraschino, one-third green chartreuse, one-third brandy. Be careful to keep the liqueurs in separate layers.

Scotch Whiskey and Soda.

Place a lump of ice in a long thin glass, add one jigger of Scotch whiskey and a bottle of cold plain soda.

Shandy Gaff.

In a glass pitcher mix one pint of Bass ale with one bottle of imported ginger ale, or fill a glass half-full of ale, then fill with ginger ale.

Sherry and Bitters.

Two dashes of Peyschaud or Angostura bitters in a sherry-glass, twist the glass until inside is covered, then fill with sherry.

Sherry and Egg.

Pour a little sherry into a fancy claret or sour-glass, add a fresh egg (be very careful not to break the yolk), then fill up with sherry.

Columbia Skin.

Put a small bar-spoon and a piece of twisted lemon-peel into a whiskey-glass, add one jigger whiskey, and fill the glass with hot water.

Scotch Whiskey Skin.

Prepare in the same manner as Columbia Skin, using Scotch whiskey.

Whiskey Skin.

Prepare same as Columbia Skin, the two being the same, only known by the two different names.

Brandy Sling (Cold).

Dissolve one lump sugar in a little water in a whiskey-glass, add a lump of ice and a jigger of brandy; mix well, and grate nutmeg on top.

Gin Sling (Cold).

Prepare same as Cold Brandy Sling, substituting gin for brandy.

Scotch Whiskey Sling (Cold).

Is made same as Cold Brandy Sling, using Scotch whiskey in place of brandy.

Whiskey Sling (Cold).

Concoct same as Cold Brandy Sling, substituting plain whiskey for brandy.

Brandy Smash (No. 1).

Dissolve one lump of sugar in a mixing-glass with a little water, add a few sprigs of fresh mint, press them gently with a muddler to extract flavor, fill the glass three-fourths full of fine ice, add one jigger brandy; mix well. Take an old-fashioned champagne glass, place a sprig of mint, stem down, in the hollow stem of glass, trim with fruit, then strain the mixture into the prepared glass.

Brandy Smash (No. 2).

Prepare same as Brandy Smash No. 1, but serve on ice same as Brandy Julep, and add a dash of Jamaica rum before serving.

Gin Smash (Strained).

Prepare in precisely the same manner as Brandy Smash No. 1, substituting gin for brandy.

Gin Smash (on Ice).

Prepare same as strained Gin Smash, leave on ice, and serve in the same manner as Gin Julep.

Medford Rum Smash.

Prepare and serve in the same manner as Brandy Smash No 1, substituting Medford rum for brandy.

Whiskey Smash.

Mix same as Brandy Smash No 1, using whiskey in place of brandy.

Snowball.

In a large mixing-glass put one pony brandy or fine whiskey, add one-half tablespoonful fine sugar, one fresh egg, fill the glass half-full fine ice; shake well, and strain into a long thin punch-glass, fill up with cold imported ginger ale. Stir and serve.

Apple Brandy Sour.

A mixing-glass half-full fine ice, add three dashes gum syrup, the juice of one-fourth of a lemon, one jigger apple brandy; mix well, strain into sour-glass, trim with fruit.

Brandy Sour.

Prepare same as Apple Brandy Sour, substituting brandy for apple brandy.

Champagne Sour.

Saturate a lump of loaf-sugar with lemon juice, put into a long thin half-pint glass, add a piece of ice and a slice of lemon, fill up with cold champagne, stir and serve.

Continental Sour.

Make a plain sour of the desired liquor and top off with claret.

Gin Sour.

Prepare same as Brandy Sour, using gin in place of brandy.

Jersey Sour.

Mix same as Apple Brandy Sour, using half a tablespoonful fine sugar in place of gum syrup.

Medford Rum Sour.

Concoct in same manner as Brandy Sour, substituting Medford rum for brandy.

St. Croix Sour.

Same as Medford, substituting St. Croix rum.

Whiskey Sour.

Prepare in same way as plain Brandy Sour, using whiskey in place of brandy.

Split Turkay.

Put the white of one egg into a mixing-glass, add half a tablespoonful fine sugar, the juice of one-fourth of a lemon, one jigger Tom gin, one jigger Italian vermouth, fill with fine ice; shake well, strain into two long bar-glasses, and fill up with cold carbonic or seltzer water. This is a pleasant ladies' drink.

Stone Fence.

Serve plain whiskey or apple brandy with cider on the side.

Stone Wall.

One lump of ice in a long thin punch-glass, one bar-spoonful fine sugar, one jigger of whiskey, add a bottle of cold plain soda; stir and drink during effervescence.

Tam o' Shanter.

Heat half a pint of ale to the boiling point, pour into a mug, add one teaspoonful fine sugar and one jigger of brandy; mix and grate a little nutmeg on top.

Syllabub.

The juice and grated outer skin of a large lemon, four glasses Rhine-wine, a quarter of a pound of sifted fine sugar. Mix the above, and let them stand some hours; then whip it, adding a pint of thick cream and the whites of two eggs cut to a froth.

Gum Syrup.

To two pounds of cut-loaf sugar add one quart of boiling water, stir until dissolved, strain, and when cold it is ready for use.

Raspberry Syrup.

Take equal parts of raspberry juice and plain syrup, put on the fire and let it come to the boiling point, strain through a thin cloth; when cold bottle and keep in a cool place.

Frappe Beef-Tea.

Dissolve a bar-spoonful of extract of beef in two jiggers of water, season to taste with celery bitters, pepper and salt, pour into a long thin glass, fill with fine ice; mix well, when cold. Sip with straws.

Brandy Toddy (Cold).

One lump of sugar dissolved with a little water in a whiskey-glass, add one lump of ice, one jigger brandy, a small piece twisted lemon-peel; mix with small bar-spoon; leave the spoon in the glass. Serve.

Brandy Toddy (Soft).

Fill a mixing-glass half-full of fine ice, add half a tablespoonful fine sugar, a little water, one jigger of brandy, a piece twisted lemon-peel; mix well with shaker, strain into sour-glass. Serve.

Gin Toddy (Cold).

Prepare in the same manner as Cold Brandy Toddy, substituting gin for brandy.

Gin Toddy (Soft).

Mix same as Soft Brandy Toddy, substituting gin for brandy.

Kentucky Toddy.

Dissolve one lump of sugar with a little water in a Briggs House glass, add one lump of ice about the size of an egg, one piece twisted lemon peel, one jigger Bourbon whiskey; mix with small barspoon, leave the spoon in the glass, grate a little nutmeg on top, and serve.

Southern Toddy.

Prepare this the same as Kentucky Toddy, which it is, but is called for by some by the above name.

Whiskey Toddy (Cold).

Prepare the same as Cold Brandy Toddy, substituting whiskey for brandy.

Tom and Jerry Mixture.

Take the whites of any quantity of eggs and beat to a stiff froth. Add one heaping tablespoonful of fine sugar for each egg. Beat the yolks of the eggs separately; mix together, adding a pinch of bicarbonate of soda, and beat to a stiff batter. Stir frequently so as to prevent the sugar from settling in the bottom of Tom and Jerry bowl.

How to Serve Tom and Jerry.

Put two tablespoonfuls of the above mixture into a Tom and Jerry mug; add half a jigger brandy and half a jigger rum, fill with boiling hot water or hot milk; mix well with a spoon, grate nutmeg on top and serve.

Tom and Jerry (Cold).

Serve same as above, using cold water or milk in place of hot.

Velvet.

Put a good-sized piece of ice into a glass pitcher, pour in at the same time one cold bottle Guinness' stout and a cold pint of champagne; stir, and serve in champagne glasses.

Vermouth and Bitters.

Serve in the same manner as Sherry and Bitters, substituting vermouth for sherry.

Raspberry Vinegar.

Put four quarts of red raspberries and five pints of white vinegar into a jar, let them stand for five days, then strain through a fine sieve, add one pound of cut-loaf sugar, boil for twenty minutes, stirring well; when cold, bottle, cork, and keep in a cool place.

Wassail Bowl.

Bake two choice apples, cut them into quarters, place them in the bottom of a punch-bowl, add two tablespoonfuls of fine sugar, one tablespoonful of allspice, the juice and peel of one lemon, one quart of hot ale, and one pint of warm sherry; mix well and serve hot.

White Plush.

In a mixing-glass half-full of fine ice put one jigger Tom gin, one pony maraschino, fill up with fresh cream or milk; shake until very cold and frothy, then strain.

Widow's Kiss.

A mixing-glass half-full fine ice, two dashes Angostura bitters, one-half a pony yellow chartreuse, one-half a pony benedictine, one pony of apple brandy; shake well, strain into a fancy cocktail-glass, and serve.

FROZEN BEVERAGES,

SUCH AS

WATER ICES, SHERBETS, AND FROZEN PUNCHES.

Certain distinctions have been made in water ices. The varieties made with fruit juice, water, and sugar only are called water ices. Those with the addition of the whites of eggs are called sherbets.

Sherbets which are of a smooth, fine texture, but only half frozen, are sometimes called sorbets.

Water ices only half frozen, without stirring, and having a rough, icy texture, are called granites.

Frozen punches are made by adding liquor to the ices either before or after freezing.

Lemon Ice.

To one pound and a quarter of fine sugar add three pints of water, the juice of ten lemons. Boil the sugar and water together twenty-five minutes, then add the lemon-juice; mix, strain, and freeze.

Orange Ice.

Three pints of water, one pound of sugar, five or six sweet oranges, according to size, the juice of one lemon. Make a hot, thick syrup of sugar and very little water. Peel half the oranges, divide them each in twelve or more parts by natural divisions, and drop the pieces of oranges in the boiling syrup. Grate the yellow part of the skin of the other three oranges in a bowl. Squeeze in the juice of the other oranges, add the syrup from the scalded orange slices, add water and lemon-juice to this syrup; mix, strain, and freeze; when half-finished stir in the sugared fruit.

Pineapple Water Ice.

Cut a ripe medium-sized pineapple in pieces, put in a jar or small tub and crush well; then put through a strainer; add to the juice obtained three quarts water and three pounds of fine sugar; mix and freeze.

Strawberry Water Ice.

Place the berries in a kettle over the fire; to each quart of berries add a full quart of water, and boil; then strain through fine sieve or cheesecloth.

Add one pound of sugar to each quart of juice obtained; allow it to cool, then freeze.

Raspberry Water Ice.

Is made in the same manner as strawberry, substituting raspberries.

Water Ice.

Three oranges, three lemons, and two pounds of sugar are to be used for each half-gallon of water. Cut the fruit into quarters, leaving the peels on, mash or crush well in a jar or tub; squeeze through a strainer; mix the juice obtained with the water and sugar thoroughly, then freeze.

Bonanza Punch.

Five quarts of water, four and a half pounds of fine sugar, the juice of twelve lemons and three oranges, one can pineapple, one-half pint of Tom gin and one pint of Rhine wine. Grate the rinds of three lemons and two oranges into a bowl, adding the juice of all. Put two quarts of water, two pounds of fine sugar, and the juice of pineapple on the fire and make a hot syrup of it. Pour this on the grated rinds and juice to draw flavor. Chop the pineapple very fine, and add to the mixture. Mix and strain all into freezer, add remainder of sugar, water; add gin and wine, and freeze.

Kirsch Punch.

Mix two quarts water, three pounds sugar, the juice of four lemons and one pint Kirschwasser. Put in freezer. When nearly frozen, whip eight whites of eggs firm; mix in and freeze again.

Egg-Nogg Frappé.

Beat two eggs until light and creamy, add two tablespoonfuls fine sugar, beat again, then add half a jigger St. Croix rum and half a jigger brandy, one pint cream or rich milk; mix well and freeze.

Grape Sherbet.

Place two pounds of washed Concord grapes in a bowl and mash them thoroughly, squeeze out all the juice through a cheesecloth or a fine sieve; add an equal amount of cold water, the juice of two lemons, use sugar enough to sweeten, and freeze.

Tea Punch Frappé.

Prepare one quart of tea, sweeten to taste, strain, and when cold add the juice of one lemon, one jigger of Jamaica rum, and one jigger of brandy; mix and freeze until mushy.

Lemon Sherbet.

Use two quarts boiling water, eight lemons, the white of an egg, one quart sugar. Spread part of the sugar on a board, and after wiping the lemons with a damp cloth roll them in the sugar to extract the oil; then cut in halves, remove the seeds and squeeze out the juice. Boil all the sugar and water until clear. Remove the scum as it rises. Add the lemon-juice to the syrup, strain it and pour gradually on to the beaten white of an egg; mix and freeze.

Lemon Ginger Sherbet.

Use one quart boiling water, one pint sugar, four lemons and four ounces of candied ginger cut in fine pieces. Shave off the peel from two lemons in thin parings; be careful not to get any of the lighter colored rind below the cells. Put the parings into a bowl, add the boiling water, and let it stand ten minutes, closely covered. Cut the lemons in halves, squeeze out the juice and steep the finely cut ginger into it; then add all the sugar to the water. When cold strain and freeze.

Pomegranate Sherbet.

Peel one dozen blood oranges, cut them in halves across the sections, remove the seeds and squeeze out the juice with a lemon squeezer. Add one pint of fine sugar and one quart water. Mix until the sugar is dissolved, then strain and freeze.

Punch à la Vatican.

Prepare a pineapple sherbet made tart with lemon-juice. Peel the lemons before squeezing so as not to get any of the oil of the rind into the juice. Mix the strained juice with the sherbet and freeze. Just before the punch is to be served add and mix into it one-half pint of old Jamaica rum and one pint of champagne for every two quarts of the sherbet.

Raspberry Sherbet.

Mash enough berries to make one pint of juice, add one pint of fine sugar, the juice of one lemon, and one pint boiling water; when the sugar is dissolved, strain the mixture through a cheesecloth or fine sieve and freeze.

Shaddock, or Grape Fruit Sherbet.

Soak one tablespoonful gelatin in a little cold water; take one pint of water and one pint fine sugar, boil for five minutes. Dissolve the soaked gelatin in the boiling syrup. Divide six shaddocks in halves across the sections, remove the seeds, and scoop out the pulp with a teaspoon. Leave all the membranous walls of the sections in the peel. Add the pulp to the cold syrup. Mix and freeze until mushy or hard, as preferred.

Strawberry Sherbet.

Prepare same as raspberry sherbet, using strawberries in place of raspberries.

Macedoine No. 1.

One-half pint currant juice, one-half pint raspberry juice. Use as much water as fruit juice; make the mixture very sweet with fine sugar and freeze.

Macedoine No. 2.

One-half pint strawberry juice, one-half pint cherry and one-half pint currant juice; sweeten and freeze.

Macedoine No. 3.

One pint orange juice, one pint pineapple, and one-half pint lemon juice; sweeten and freeze same as Macedoine No. 1.

Macedoine No. 4.

One pint plum and one pint grape juice; sweeten and freeze same as the other Macedoines.

Orange Sherbet No. 1.

Boil three pints of water and one and a half pints fine sugar together for twenty minutes. Add the juice of twenty oranges and one lemon; mix well, strain, and freeze.

Orange Sherbet No. 2.

Use one pint cold water, one pint strained orange juice, one-half pint fine sugar, one tablespoonful gelatin, and one-quarter of a pint boiling water. Soak the gelatin in one-quarter of a pint of the cold water for ten minutes. Put the sugar and remainder of water into a bowl, add the orange juice. Dissolve the gelatin in the boiling water and add it to the mixture; stir well, strain, and freeze.

Pine Apple Sherbet.

A pint and a half canned, or one large ripe pineapple, a pint of fine sugar, a pint of water, one tablespoonful gelatin. Soak the gelatin one hour in cold water. Cut the hearts and eyes from the fruit, chop it fine, add the sugar and juice of fruit. Have half of the water hot, and dissolve the gelatin in it, stir this and the cold water into the chopped pineapple and freeze.

Roman Punch.

Mix three pounds of fine sugar, three quarts water, the juice of eight lemons, one-fourth pint brandy, one-fourth pint Jamaica rum, one pony curaçoa; strain, mix in the beaten whites of eight eggs, and freeze.

Russian Punch.

Squeeze the juice of eight lemons into a bowl, add three quarts water and three pounds of fine sugar, mix and strain into freezer; add half a pint allash, a quarter of a pint orange brandy, and the whites of six eggs well beaten; stir and freeze.

Blackberry Sherbet.

One quart of ripe berries or enough to make one pint of juice, one pint of fine sugar, the juice of one lemon. Mash the berries, add the sugar, and after the sugar is dissolved add the water and lemon-juice. Press through a fine cheesecloth or sieve, and freeze.

Cherry Sherbet.

One pound of fine sugar, one pint fruit juice, one pint boiling water. Mash the cherries and strain out the juice. Boil the sugar and water five minutes, remove the scum, and strain through a fine cheesecloth or sieve; when cool add the fruit juice and freeze.

Currant Sherbet No. 1.

Prepare same as Cherry Sherbet, using one pint of currant juice in place of cherry.

Currant Sherbet No. 2.

One pint sugar, one quart of water, one pint of currant juice, the juice of one lemon. Boil the water and sugar together half an hour. Add the currant and lemon juice to the syrup. Let this cool and freeze.

Café Royal Frappé.

To two quarts clear strong coffee add half a pint cognac, sweeten to taste, put in freezer, and freeze until mushy.

JOHN L. STODDARD'S POPULAR PICTORIALS

GLIMPSES OF THE WORLD

Hundreds of full-page views portraying scenes all over the world, taken from photographs collected by the celebrated traveler and lecturer, John L. Stoddard, who has charmingly described each one. 550 pages; paper of the richest and heaviest quality; size 11x14 inches. Unquestionably the finest work of the kind ever published.

English Edition:

- Buckram, Chemograph $6.00
- Buckram, Half-Tone 4.50
- Full Morocco, Half-Tone, Gold Stamped ... 7.50

German Edition:

- Green Silk Cloth Binding, Gold Stamped ... 3.50

Spanish Edition:

- Silk Cloth Binding, Gold Stamped 3.50
- Full Morocco, Gold Stamped 7.50

FROM THE ATLANTIC TO THE PACIFIC

A grand panorama of famous scenes and noted places on our own Continent. Most interesting to the student of Art, Science, or Literature. Read this page of the world's history first; be familiar with your own country. Cloth bound, extra quality enameled paper printed on one side of leaf only. Stamped in two colors. Price, $2.00.

SUNNY LANDS OF THE EASTERN CONTINENT

A pictorial journey through the tropical countries of the Old World, containing the choicest views from Italy, Greece, Turkey, India, Syria, Palestine, China, Japan, Egypt, Africa, Australia, etc. People interested in missionary work should possess this volume. Handsomely bound in cloth; 128 pages; enameled paper; special cover design in two colors. Price, $2.00.

FAMOUS PARKS AND PUBLIC BUILDINGS OF AMERICA

One hundred and twenty-eight full-page views of the marvelous works of Nature in the New World. To those who have seen these grand originals, these pictures will prove charming souvenirs, and cannot fail to be interesting to all Americans. Bound in cloth. Only one side of page utilized. Enameled paper. Cover design stamped in two colors. Price, $2.00.

A TOUR THROUGH NORTHERN EUROPE

A rare and elaborate collection of 128 views in the historic countries of Europe—a pictorial history of accomplished and fascinating races. A book of inestimable value when used in connection with the studies of History and Geography. Cloth bound. Stamped in two colors. Enameled paper. Price, $2.00.

Any of the above Books sent postpaid upon receipt of price by

THE SAALFIELD PUBLISHING COMPANY, AKRON, OHIO.

THE FAMOUS OTIS BOOKS FOR BOYS

James Otis, the Popular Juvenile Writer, needs no introduction to the boys of to-day.

TELEGRAPH TOM'S VENTURE

A highly entertaining story of a boy who assisted a United States officer of the law in working up a famous case. The narrative is both interesting and instructive in that it shows what a bright boy can accomplish when thrown upon his own resources. Throughout an intensely interesting and exciting story. 228 pages.

MESSENGER NO. 48

Relates the experiences of a faithful messenger boy in a large city, who, in answering a call was the means of ferreting out a band of criminals who for years had baffled the police and detectives. The story tells of the many dangers and hardships these boys have to undergo; the important services they often render by their clever movements; and how by his fidelity to duty, Messenger Boy No. 48 rose to a most important position of trust and honor. It teaches boys that self-reliance, pluck, and the faithful performance of duties are the real secret of success. 241 pages.

DOWN THE SLOPE

The hero of this story is a boy, who, in order to assist his mother, works as "breaker" in a coal mine. The book tells how coal miners work; their social condition; their hardships and privations; and the older reader will get an excellent idea of the causes of labor troubles in this industry, and will become more sympathetic toward this class of people. The young readers will find in this book a high ideal of a boy's devotion to his mother, and will learn how manly courage and a brave heart will overcome great difficulties, and lead to success and honor. 273 pages.

TEDDY

A captivating story of how Teddy, a village boy, helped to raise the mortgage on his mother's home, and the means he took for doing so. The obstacles his crabbed uncle placed in his way; his connection with the fakirs at the county fair; his successful cane and knife board; his queer lot of friends and how they aided him; and how he finally outwitted his enemies, are all set forth so clearly and attractively in this volume that we forget that the hero is not a real boy, and his trials and successes real occurrences. The characters are taken from life, Mr. Otis himself acting as "fakir" in order to become thoroughly acquainted with the surroundings. "Teddy" is sure to win a warm place in the hearts of all boy readers. 293 pages.

All of the above are bound in cloth, have special cover designs in two colors, with titles stamped in gold; illustrated; 12mo.

Price, 75c. each.

Any of the above Books sent postpaid upon receipt of price by

THE SAALFIELD PUBLISHING COMPANY, AKRON, OHIO.

BOOKS BY THOMAS W. KNOX

Who, as a Juvenile Writer, has held a prominent place among the very best writers of boys' books in the world.

BOYS' LIFE OF GENERAL GRANT

Illustrated; large, square 12mo. Cloth binding. 420 pages. This account of our great General begins with the arrival of his ancestors on American soil; follows him through his childhood; his career at West Point, and active military career thereafter. It will give the boy reader a clear idea of the Mexican War, and quite a full account of the War of the Rebellion. The General's voyage around the world also enlivens the narrative. Told in the spirited and absorbing way that Mr. Knox has of writing for boy readers.

THE LOST ARMY

A story illustrative of the camp and military life of the soldiers of the Federal Army in the Civil War.

"It is a stirring, well-told narrative of patriotic adventure and service, and will kindle the love of Country and Humanity in the young reader."
—*Congregationalist.*

"It is full of stirring incidents."—*San Francisco Chronicle.*

Cloth bound, with emblematic cover design; illustrated.

CAPTAIN JOHN CRANE

The hero of this book tells his adventures on the sea from 1800 to 1815; his experiences with the pirates; the dangers of our ships during the trouble with France and Tripoli; how British war ships overhauled our merchantmen; their manner of searching for deserters, etc., etc. Sailors' superstitions are woven into the narrative in the most admirable manner. The story is historically correct and entertainingly related. Handsomely bound in cloth, stamped in two colors, 311 pages.

A CLOSE SHAVE

Or how Major Flagg won his bet, and journeyed around the world in seventy days. Modern aids to travel and communication; valuable scientific discoveries and inventions brought to the reader's attention in an attractive form. The routes, time-tables, monsoons, etc., described in "A Close Shave" may be relied upon as being absolutely correct. An excellent description of the country between New York and San Francisco; a train robbery with one of the notorious Jesse James gang as a leader; an exciting experience with a school of whales; a typhoon and the wreck; the story about monsoons; Chinese and Malay pirates; a train accident in Egypt, etc., etc. Will prove exceedingly interesting to all boy readers. Cloth bound. Special cover design. Illustrated.

THE TALKING HANDKERCHIEF

Under this title, Colonel Knox, that inveterate globe-trotter and writer of stories for boys, has gathered a collection of absorbing tales of adventure in Russia, China, India, and elsewhere, which will prove of deep interest to both young and old. Cloth bound; illustrated with over one hundred drawings by John Henderson Garnsey. 12mo.

Price, $1.25 each.

Any of the above Books sent postpaid upon receipt of price by

THE SAALFIELD PUBLISHING COMPANY, AKRON, OHIO.

THE BOY CAPTAIN

By CAPTAIN NAUTILUS (C. E. Eldridge). This is a unique story for boys, written in a most interesting and engrossing style. It tells in a graphic manner of the adventurous life of a boy who assumed command of a small trading vessel, making trips between the United States and South American ports. Being unusual and new in plot, "The Boy Captain" should prove a delight to both boys and girls. Cloth bound; artistic cover design; stamped in gold and inks. 268 pages. Price, 75c.

THE FIRST CAPTURE

By HARRY CASTLEMON, author of "Gunboat Series," "Sportsman Club Series," etc. A thrilling story of the Revolutionary War, beginning with the first capture of a British schooner in the harbor of a New England town. Told in the author's most charming style. You at once catch the spirit of "Ye Olden Days," and glimpses of the way the people lived, how they were governed, and how "Justice" was administered. Bound in cloth, special cover design in gold and inks. 12mo. Price, 75c.

MARKING THE BOUNDARY

By EDWARD E. BILLINGS. Illustrated. 12mo. Cloth. A comparatively fresh subject has been here chosen. The story opens with the setting out of the expedition to finish laying off the forty-ninth parallel, which is part of the boundary line between the United States and the British Provinces. Price, 75c.

THE ROMANCE OF A SCHOOL BOY

By MARY A. DENISON. Illustrated. 12mo. Cloth. "The Romance of a School Boy" is unobjectionable in moral tone; its tendency is to elevate and ennoble; and it is full of interesting adventures, thrilling situations, and pretty romance. Price, 75c.

THE CASTLE OF THE CARPATHIANS

By JULES VERNE. Illustrated, large, square 12mo. Cloth. The very name of the author is enough to attract any one to this book. The descriptions of the quaint villagers of Werst, their costumes, manner of living, and belief in the supernatural would in themselves prove an interesting narrative, but when coupled with the exciting adventures of Nic Deck, the two Counts, the cowardly Doctor, and the beautiful La Stilla, the story is undoubtedly one of the most enchanting ever offered to young readers. Price, 75c.

Any of the above Books sent postpaid upon receipt of price by

THE SAALFIELD PUBLISHING COMPANY, AKRON, OHIO.

Classic Cocktail Guides and Retro Bartender Books

CHILDREN'S BIBLE STORIES

By JOSEPHINE POLLARD, one of the most charming and successful writers of children's books, whose songs are used in all our Sunday Schools.

TITLES:
- **GOD MADE THE WORLD**
- **RUTH, A BIBLE HEROINE**
- **THE GOOD SAMARITAN**
- **THE BOYHOOD OF JESUS**
- **THE STORY OF JESUS TOLD IN PICTURES**

A series of five volumes comprising the sweet stories of God's Word told in simple language so the little ones themselves can read them and learn to prize them as the best of all books. They combine entertainment and moral instruction in the most fascinating manner, and will cultivate the child's taste for that which is beautiful and ennobling. To the young reader they make the Bible seem like a new book. Each volume is complete; is illustrated with scores of magnificent engravings; is printed on fine paper in large clear type, having words of more than one syllable divided so they may be easily pronounced by children; bound in cloth with emblematic cover designs, attractively stamped in three bright colors.

Price, 75c. each.

YOUNG PEOPLE'S BIBLE STORIES

By JOSEPHINE POLLARD.

TITLES:
- **HISTORY OF THE OLD TESTAMENT**
- **HISTORY OF THE NEW TESTAMENT**
- **BIBLE STORIES FOR CHILDREN**
- **SWEET STORY OF GOD**

A series of four volumes containing historic incidents from the Bible. They make a continuous record of the Old and New Dispensations, omitting all that is too abstract for young readers. The boys and girls reading these volumes will not only obtain the religious truths they need, but will also unconsciously derive invaluable lessons in the simplicity and power of their English mother-tongue. All are works of untold interest, and will prove a powerful influence for good in every home. Each volume contains a colored frontispiece, is profusely illustrated, printed in large, clear type on super-calendered paper, bound in cloth, with special cover designs in three brilliant colors, titles in gold.

Price, $1.25 each.

Any of the above Books sent postpaid upon receipt of price by

THE SAALFIELD PUBLISHING COMPANY, AKRON, OHIO.

MR. BUNNY, HIS BOOK

By ADAH L. SUTTON. Illustrated by W. H. Fry. The finest juvenile on the market. Just published. Far superior to anything of the kind ever before presented to the little ones. Sure to attract and delight the children.

The Quaint Characters, Comical Situations, Laughable Incidents, Queer Episodes, Ridiculous Personages, Catchy Rhymes, Bright Sayings and Brilliant Colors — To be found in "Mr. Bunny, His Book," will bring forth hearty laughter and attract and interest the little ones, proving an unfailing source of enjoyment to them.

Over 100 pages; 9x11½ inches; board covers; substantially and durably bound; front and back cover designs stamped in three colors; printed on good, strong paper, large faced type, easily read. Every story fully illustrated. Each page printed in three bright colors.

Price, $1.25.

LIVING PICTURES FROM THE ANIMAL KINGDOM

By DR. L. HECK. A superb pictorial, showing reproductions of photographs of the rarest and finest specimens of the animal kingdom, *taken from life*. Heretofore those interested in the study of animal life were confined to dull descriptions with no object lessons whatsoever; therefore this book, "LIVING PICTURES FROM THE ANIMAL KINGDOM," will undoubtedly greatly enhance interest in this branch of science, proving of inestimable value to the professor and student of zoölogy.

Every member of the household will welcome this beautiful book, for animal pictures of the size shown therein are a novelty. The foot-notes describing the habits, etc., of the originals of the lifelike illustrations will be found exceedingly interesting. Emblematic cover design, stamped in gold. Size, 11x14 inches. Over 200 pages. Printed on heavy enameled paper.

Cloth, $3.00; Full Morocco, $4.50.

Any of the above Books sent postpaid upon receipt of price by

THE SAALFIELD PUBLISHING COMPANY, AKRON, OHIO.

Classic Cocktail Guides and Retro Bartender Books

YOUNG PEOPLE'S LIBRARY

A series of ten volumes, selected from the best works of the most popular authors. Bound in cloth with artistic cover designs stamped in three colors. No two alike. 12mo.

Price, 50c. each.

TITLES:

THE STORY OF ELECTRICITY FOR AMATEURS AND STUDENTS
By JAMES W. STEELE. The greatest facts of the present civilization set forth in a clear manner. Many illustrations and diagrams.

THE ART OF GOOD MANNERS
By SHIRLEY DARE. Lessons in regard to etiquette taught by this little book will be remembered long on account of the charming manner in which they are presented.

SOME QUEER AMERICANS
A gossipy sketch of the queer characters to be found in the Blue Ridge, their costumes, manner of living, and speaking.

MR. SWEET POTATOES
A story of a Chinese Milkman.

A NIGHT WITH PAUL BOYTON
An interesting experience with this noted sailor on a Florida River, with descriptions of the quaint costumes worn on this excursion.

MILTON'S MULBERRY TREE
Near the College at Cambridge, and the care it receives. Also five stories of Colonial life, "Murillo's Boy," etc.

A QUEER LETTER-CARRIER
A Massachusetts letter-carrier whose route was between two forts during the Revolutionary War.

THE RAGAMUFFINS AND GENERAL WASHINGTON
An attractive story for young patriots.

BUSINESS OPENINGS FOR GIRLS
By SALLIE JOY WHITE. A pure, earnest talk with girls.

A BOY'S RACE WITH GENERAL GRANT
A glowing description of a race on the plains of Turkey between Gen. Grant and the son of the American Consul.

Any of the above Books sent postpaid upon receipt of price by

THE SAALFIELD PUBLISHING COMPANY, AKRON, OHIO.

Classic Cocktail Resource Guide

Some ingredients found in vintage cocktail guides are unavailable or hard to come by today. However, the creation of historically accurate cocktails is a growing hobby and with a bit of Internet research, you will find recipes for bitters and syrups online, as well as manufacturers that are developing new product lines for the classic cocktail enthusiast.

Vendors

A short selection of online vendors selling bitters, mixers, syrups, wine, liqueurs, and spirits. This list is by no means complete but is a good place to start your search.

BevMo!
www.bevmo.com

Binny's Beverage Depot
www.binnys.com

The Bitter Truth
www.the-bitter-truth.com

Cocktail Kingdom
www.cocktailkingdom.com

Fee Brothers
www.feebrothers.com

Hi-Time Wine Cellars
www.hitimewine.net

Internet Wines and Spirits
www.internetwines.com

The Jug Shop
www.thejugshop.com

Monin Gourmet Flavorings
www.moninstore.com

Trader Tiki's Hand-Crafted Exotic Syrups
www.tradertiki.com

The Whiskey Exchange
www.thewhiskyexchange.com

General Interest

These sites provide background information on individual ingredients, suggestions for substitutes, current commercial availability, and recipes.

The Chanticleer Society
A Worldwide Organization of Cocktail Enthusiasts
www.chanticleersociety.org

Drink Boy
Adventures in Cocktails
www.drinkboy.com

The Internet Cocktail Database Ingredients Search
www.cocktaildb.com/ingr_search

Museum of the American Cocktail
www.museumoftheamericancocktail.org

WebTender Wiki
www.wiki.webtender.com

Classic Cocktail Guides and Retro Bartender Books

Coming Soon from
Classic Cocktail Guides
and Retro Bartender Books

Home Made Beverages

The Manufacture of Non-Alcoholic and
Alcoholic Drinks in the Household, Including
Recipes for Essences, Extracts, and Syrups

A Pre-Prohibition Cocktail Book

Albert Hopkins

Classic Cocktail Guides
and Retro Bartender Books

American and Other Drinks

Recipes for Making the Principal Beverages
Used in the United States and Elsewhere:
A Nineteenth-Century Cocktail Guide

Leo Engel

ISBN: 978-1-880954-37-9

Classic Cocktail Guides
and Retro Bartender Books

Oxford Night Caps

A Collection of Recipes for
Making Various Cups, Beverages,
and Cocktails Used in the University

Richard Cook

ISBN: 978-1-880954-38-6

Classic Cocktail Guides
and Retro Bartender Books

Cups and Their Customs

A Study in Bacchanology with Recipes for Cocktails and Mixed Drinks of the 1800s

Henry Porter
and George Edwin Roberts

ISBN: 978-1-880954-39-3

Now Available from
Historic Cookbooks of the World

Recipes of Sweden

A Classic Swedish Cookbook

Compiled by
Inga Norberg

ISBN: 978-1-880954-27-0

Now Available from
Historic Cookbooks of the World

Recipes of the Highlands and Islands of Scotland

A Classic Scottish Cookbook

Compiled by
An Comunn Gaidhealach

Originally published as
"The Feill Cookery Book"

ISBN: 978-1-880954-25-6

www.ingramcontent.com/pod-product-compliance
Lightning Source LLC
Chambersburg PA
CBHW031447040426
42444CB00007B/1013